Spiritual Trends
and
Modern Movements

Discipleship Movement?
Healing Movement?
Deliverance Movement?
Faith Movement?
Prosperity Movement?
Church Growth Movement?
Kingdom Movement?
Dominion Movement?
Worship Movement?
        Etc. Etc. Etc.

- How does the believer sort through all of the movements?

- Where is the church headed?

- How can we stay in the mainstream?

- How do we avoid possible deception?

- How can we balance the new with the old?

In this book Pastor Iverson, a man known for his balance, shares personal insights and biblical principles that will help church members and leaders alike to maintain their spiritual footing as the winds of doctrine blow.

MAINTAINING

BALANCE

WHEN WINDS OF DOCTRINE BLOW

MAINTAINING

BALANCE

WHEN WINDS OF DOCTRINE BLOW

MAINTAINING

BALANCE

WHEN WINDS OF DOCTRINE BLOW

Dick Iverson

AVAILABLE FROM:

BIBLE TEMPLE PUBLISHING
7545 NE GLISAN STREET
PORTLAND, OREGON 97213
1-800-777-6057

Paperback ISBN 0-914936-80-8
Hardback ISBN 0-914936-81-6

PRINTED IN U.S.A.

CONTENTS

ACKNOWLEDGEMENT

I would like to recognize two people who played a key role in the development of this book.

A dear brother in our church, Ray Grant, took the original messages that I gave at pastors' conferences and spent many hours working on the first manuscript.

Bill Scheidler, an elder and teacher in our church, sacrificed hours more to polish up the manuscript and make this final copy ready.

I wish to express my deep appreciation to these two men for their labor of love.

Maintaining
BALANCE
when winds
of
doctrine
blow

PREFACE

After having pastored for nearly twenty-five years myself, my heart goes out to those pastors who are trying with all their strength to maintain a smooth-running local church that will bring glory to the name of Christ. I understand about all the struggles, the disappointments, and the temptations to give up on the sheep at times. I have also experienced the joy of seeing God change lives, and the excitement of watching God bring deliverance to many souls.

During these years I have seen many local churches, which have started from humble beginnings, go on and become a major influence for good in their various communities. When I see that, I share their deep joy and sense of accomplishment. My spirit joins in with their satisfaction of a job well done.

But on the other hand, I have also been saddened by the sight of churches that once were moving in the truth and power of God

Maintaining
BALANCE
when winds
of
doctrine
blow

suddenly come to nothing. They have lost their
influence, their sheep have been scattered, and
their ministers are shipwrecked.

I have often wondered, what made the
difference? What was it that would cause some
churches to succeed and others to fail? Some
to abound to the glory of God, and others to
bring reproach to the Gospel? As a pastor of
a church these things have greatly concerned
me. Because if these kind of things were
happening to other churches, then how could
I be certain our local church might not end
up in shipwreck?

What could be done to prevent failure?
Are there any guidelines or principles that
would help insure a church's standing strong in
the will of God? What is the key to success in
pastoring a "permanent" church?

From many years of personal experience
in pastoring and also from hosting a regional
ministers' conference for many years, I have
seen a pattern develop. A pattern, which when
followed brings stability to a church, and which
when ignored leads to an eventual downward
tail spin. In talking to many other shepherds,
and in being called to "trouble-shoot" many
ailing churches, a basic principle has emerged
that I have found means the difference between
success and failure. I would like to share this
insight with you in the following pages.

My deepest desire and on-going hope for you and all churches is that each local body of believers would go on and become everything that God intended for them to be. That the fullness of the glory of God would continually dwell in all of our churches, and that they would redound in praise and worship to Him!

Dick Iverson

Maintaining **BALANCE** *when winds of doctrine blow*

ONE

GAINING A BALANCED PERSPECTIVE

There are many writers, researchers, and optimistic entrepreneurs who write books claiming to have recently discovered "the answer," and "cure," the "solution," the "key" or the "secret" that anyone who wants to succeed just has to know! It may be the key to losing weight, the secret of financial success, the answer to your economic problems, the cure for the common cold or the solution to marital unhappiness.

Practically everyone has a problem of one sort or another, and these authors would have us believe they are the source of knowledge that can bring us the solutions that will enhance our living with success, prosperity, and unending happiness. And some researchers have thought up techniques or procedures that do bring some temporary relief to our problems.

On the other hand there are many quacks, "snake oil" medicine men, opportunists

Maintaining
BALANCE
*when winds
of
doctrine
blow*

and outright charlatans, who skip town as soon as they have relieved us of our money. It is important then to know your source of "wisdom"; to know by what authority that source has a right to give advice; and to find the basis for their solution, key or secret.

SUCCESSFUL CHURCH

The same is true in the area of church life. Every pastor, elder and deacon wants a successful church. It is our heart's desire to have a smooth flowing, unified congregation of believers ministering effectively to each other and to the world (Colossians 1:9-11).

We would all like to know the "secret" or "key" to having such a local church! Many men claim to know the answer and they are all eager to let us know they have the answer! One person has his solution, another has his unique program, and still another has a newly discovered technique just waiting to be revealed to the masses. We all justifiably wonder and ask, "Who is right?"

If we listen to what men say we can be sure that we are going to end up being worse off than when we started! But if we go to the tried and tested source of truth, the Word of God, we can never go wrong. It is the ministry of the Holy Spirit to open understanding to the written word so that we can know the basic principles that will insure our success in

Every pastor, elder and deacon wants a successful church

establishing a strong local church (John 14:26, 15:26). Any time we have a problem in our churches, whether it is human in origin, or diabolic, it is reassuring to be able to go to the Word and say, "It is written!" The Word of God has been given to us by God so that we can "war a good warfare" and reach God's goal for us as individuals and for the church as a corporate body. Truly, as we follow the principles that are established in the Word of God, we will find the success and prosperity that the Word promises.

DEFINING THE PROBLEM

In order to gain a better understanding of the problem that is facing many churches today and why it is so important to me as a pastor, I would like to relate some of my personal background as a pastor.

I was raised in historic Pentecostal churches. I was one of those peculiar individuals who were literally "born" in church. From the earliest of my years I can remember the hard wooden benches of our local church.

Maintaining **BALANCE** *when winds of doctrine blow*

When I was young my parents attended the Assembly of God church in Minnesota, and I was saved as a child in that church. Just before World War II our family moved to Oregon. In Oregon our family started going to the Foursquare church. It was in the Foursquare church I was filled with the Holy Spirit.

After attending the Foursquare church for a season we began attending a church nearer to our home where T.L. Osborn was then pastoring. The church was affiliated with the Church of God. As a teenager in this church I grew up under the ministry of T.L. Osborn.

Through these early years I gained a wide variety of church experience and I have to say I appreciate what God did in my life each step of the way. I appreciate my roots and I know that God wanted me to learn something important in each church I attended.

I had only been involved for a short time in this new church when my pastor, T.L. Osborn, got involved in the deliverance ministry and became an evangelist. Because of this, I also began to get involved as an evangelist. I started out watching the tent and working as a "tent boy".

At this time of my life I was still single. Little did I know at this very time that my future wife who was attending a small Foursquare church would find herself in the middle of one of the greatest outpourings of the Spirit to come in modern times. She had enrolled in a small Bible college in North Battleford, Saskatchewan where God was moving in a great spirit of revival. Signs and wonders and miracles were taking place in a powerful way.

I appreciate my roots

Because of this background it was natural for us when we did get married to travel as evangelists. We travelled in Europe and especially in the British Isles. We were involved primarily in the healing and evangelistic ministry for the next ten years. Those were exciting and productive times.

When I was in my early thirties I became an associate pastor with my father in Oregon. The Church of God where I had spent my teenage years had withdrawn from its denominational affiliation by that time and was an independent pentecostal church. As you can see, by that time I had experienced all of the major pentecostal denominations and now I was to find out what an independent church was like. I have to say that I really appreciate the background that I had. There were good times and there were bad times. There were positive experiences and there were negative experiences. But through it all God was teaching me, shaping me and maturing me for His purposes. At times I learned what to do and at other times I learned what not to do. But, praise God, I <u>was</u> learning!

BECOMING A PASTOR

At this point in my life my dad suffered a severe heart attack, and he asked me to take over the senior pastorate of the church. I had been accustomed to holding evangelistic revival meetings with thousands attending. Pastoring

Maintaining **BALANCE** *when winds of doctrine blow*

a small group of one hundred people just did not have the appeal or carry the excitement to which I had become accustomed. It did not make any sense to me to leave the evangelistic field for 100 people. The world needed me and my ministry (so I thought) and it would be a waste to be confined in this way.

My father refused to step down from the pastorate unless I came and took over. The problem was that medically speaking it was mandatory that he resign. So I reluctantly accepted the pastorate.

At first I missed the excitement of traveling, the glory of large crowds, and the pressure-less position of being a care-free evangelist. Inwardly, I had it figured that I would take the pastorate just long enough until another minister happened by who wanted the church and I would turn it over to him. God never intended for such a pastor to come. He had a different plan. During the next five years God molded and shaped me into the pastor that He wanted me to be. Those were precious growing years and times of learning in God's winepress when God made me into the vessel that conformed to His plan for my life.

God had seen the church from the foundation of the world.

IMPORTANCE OF THE CHURCH

As a pastor and a shepherd over God's flock in our locality, I began to feel God's great concern and love for His church. I began to realize how important the church was in the mind of God. Christ gave Himself for the church in a sacrificial love as precious as a husband's love for his beautiful bride (Ephesians 5:25). Christ was extremely jealous and protective over the bride and anything that harmed His church struck at His very heart.

I began to see that God had seen the church from the foundation of the world. He saw a triumphant people who were called out from Jews and Gentiles comprised of people from every nation, kindred, tribe and tongue. I began to see God's people the way in which He saw them as the apple of His eye, a peculiar treasure in the earth on which He lavished His love.

When I saw this I also understood the reason for my existence as a pastor. I was given by Christ to the church to nurture, protect and edify the people of God and help them to become all that God wanted them to become from the feeblest saint to the most ambitious, from the youngest to the oldest. God is extremely concerned about His church.

TIDES AND CURRENTS OF REVIVAL

Each additional year that I pastor I continue to grow in my appreciation for God's love for His body. My understanding of the importance of a strong local church continues

Maintaining
BALANCE
*when winds
of
doctrine
blow*

to expand. I am more and more able to see how vital the church is to the carrying out of God's purposes in the earth. How exciting it is to be part of the vast plan of God!

But each year I also am coming to a better understanding of those things that can potentially bring harm to the church and those things that hinder its growth and productivity.

Through the years our church saw many evangelists and revivalists. There have been periods of spectacular revival, times of great renewal in areas of teaching, and seasons of emphasis and re-emphasis on some basis fundamentals of church life. Along with these we have experienced all of the doctrinal waves of popular Christian movements.

We experienced the wave of truth which emphasized a greater dimension in worship. And our church was greatly blessed through this teaching. Our church began to grow dramatically as we honored God in worship. For when the Lord is lifted up, not only as the crucified Christ, but also lifted up and exalted as the reigning Lord, then men are drawn unto Him and to His body, the church (John 12:32, Philippians 2:9, Psalm 21:13). Worship gives people a point of reference for their lives in the midst of cultural turmoil, personal problems, and marital stresses. Christ is that focal point. He is the one who gives meaning to life and suffering. When He is lifted up, men and women find hope! They come and find answers.

God is extremely concerned about His church.

Following this there were other movements. There was the Charismatic movement. God was pouring out His Holy Spirit in churches of many varied denominations, backgrounds, and persuasions. From the sedate Episcopalians, to the dogmatic Baptists, to the quiet Quakers, to the formal Methodists. All over the land, God was moving in charismatic dimensions. Lives were revitalized through the emphasis on the baptism of the Holy Spirit.

Later, there was the Jesus movement during the seventies. With all its unique idiosyncrasies, and styles, many young people were redeemed from lives headed toward destruction. God also used this movement to shake churches from their lethargy and get them involved in helping hurting people outside the four walls of their church buildings.

Through the years there have been other movements as well. The "faith" movement, the discipleship movement, the prosperity movement, and on and on. Different emphases and doctrinal waves have gone throughout the land. Each wave carrying with it water to strengthen and refresh, but also at times carrying silt and sand that could potentially muddy the waters.

DEALING WITH EMPHASES

We have seen some local churches get swept up in the current of a particular

Maintaining **BALANCE** *when winds of doctrine blow*

movement and really be blessed. Others have been hurt. Some have done well for a while and then have become disillusioned, even to the point of shipwreck.

I quickly wish to insert here that I personally have been strengthened in some way by every major move of the Spirit that has come into my life. I want to remain positive about this subject. I do not care how radical, or how off-base a movement may have become, or even if it ended up in a ditch, there is some good that has come of it that has blessed my life. I could go through every one of the movements I have mentioned, and so could you, and we could find some very serious problems with each one of them.

It would be easy to react against everyone of them, and reject totally their particular emphases. We human beings often tend to be creatures of reaction. We often react because of a problem or an over emphasis, or because a truth was taken out of balance. We often reject truth because it was mishandled or misrepresented. We must guard against becoming reactionary.

I have been strengthened by every major move of the Spirit that has come into my life.

I have pastored for over a quarter of a century, and I realize that I have not learned everything there is to know about pastoring. I do not have all the answers. But I would like to share with you what I have learned about responding to the various movements and particular emphases that sweep across our church. The health of the local church is the daily concern that I carry. The people of God and their welfare are of utmost importance to me, and I am sure to you as well (II Corinthians 11:28). I am very excited about those things that will bless and uplift the church. But those things that would bring harm I get extremely nervous about.

At any point in time there are a variety of doctrinal emphases and religious movements vying for attention within the Christian community. Sooner or later they demand a response from the local leadership. How far do we go in endorsing, emphasizing, or implementing each one? I believe the key to a successful church is dependent upon how we handle and deal with these emphases.

WHY DOES IMBALANCE OCCUR?

Why does imbalance occur? Why on earth would a productive church shock us with exposed scandal or fraud? How can people be so persuaded as to get involved with some of the most bizarre deviations from biblical Christianity? How could a minister so easily lead hundreds of people to a distant jungle to die? Why would seemingly intelligent individuals in this twentieth century follow a self-acclaimed Indian guru into a barren desert valley and return with nothing to show for it? What causes a person to lose their objectivity so that the "wolf" type leader can not be seen

Maintaining
BALANCE
when winds
of
doctrine
blow

for what he is? We are not talking about events that happen somewhere else. But in today's world deception is happening to our own neighbors, to our friends and to our own fellow ministers!

Even Paul was astonished at how quickly a group of believers could be turned away from the truth:

> *"I marvel that ye are so soon removed from Him that called you into the grace of Christ unto another gospel; which is not another, but there be some that trouble you, and would pervert the gospel of Christ"* *(Galatians 1:6-7).*

No local church, and no group of believers seems to be immune from the possibility of becoming imbalanced, or moving off to the extreme on a tangent, or becoming deceived by a doctrinal truth that has been twisted beyond its proper meaning.

THE NATURE OF SHEEP

The people of God and their welfare are of utmost importance

Part of the answer as to why imbalance occurs lies in the nature of the sheep (people) and the nature of the flock (congregation). The tendency to go to extremes, from one to another arises because the sheep let their "fallen" human natures dominate their actions, rather than letting the "divine" nature, which is imparted to them by the Holy Spirit, control their thinking and actions.

When people are saved by the grace of God out of the world, they can easily bring this nature with them. Young converts are "babes in Christ." They are unskilled in handling the Word, (Hebrews 5:13). So the way they were used to handling trends and fads in the world is the same say they are now handling doctrines and new teachings in relation to their Christian life and the church. They are like children who have discovered a new exciting toy, or who are going on a new adventure for the first time. All the new doctrines are exciting and arouse a certain curiosity. They immediately chase after them until the newness wears off; and then with the same intensity they had before, they begin running in a totally different direction after another newly found truth.

New Christians and older ones who have not grown up are what the Apostle Peter calls "unstable". Since they are unstable, they become an easy prey for anyone who claims to have a new doctrine.

"But there were false prophets also among the people, even as there shall be false teachers among you, who privily shall bring in damnable heresies...beguiling <u>unstable souls</u>" (II Peter 2:1,14).

"As also in all his [Paul's] epistles, speaking in them of these things, in which are some things hard to be understood; which they that are <u>unlearned</u> and <u>unstable</u>

Maintaining **BALANCE** *when winds of doctrine blow*

wrest, as they do also the other Scriptures, unto their own destruction. Ye therefore, beloved seeing ye know these things before, beware lest ye also, being led astray with the error of the wicked, fall from your own steadfastness. (II Peter 3:16-17).

In the midst of this tendency toward instability Peter cries out for steadfastness, "Remain stable. Don't be led astray. Keep your balance!"

There is an urgency about the need for the sheep in our congregations to not live according to the old fallen human nature, but to live according to the sanctified, redeemed nature that Christ has given to them. Paul advised Christians to mortify the carnal nature, put to death the earthly nature, and walk in the Spirit (Colossians 3:5; Galatians 5:16). Self-control, steadfastness, faithfulness, and stability are all characteristics of the divine nature of which God has graciously allowed us to partake (II Peter 1:4). We will never go wrong when we conduct our lives in harmony with these godly characteristics.

Our message to the sheep in all of our congregations should be the same as that trumpeted by the author of the book to the Hebrews:

"Jesus Christ the same yesterday, today and forever. [So] be not carried about with divers and strange doctrines. For it

What causes a person to lose their objectivity

is a good thing that the heart be established with grace..." (Hebrews 13:8-9).

The <u>New English Bible</u> brings out the thought that since Jesus Christ is the same all the time no one should be swept off their course by any sort of new or extreme teaching. The sheep do well just to remain calm and collected, and keep feeding beside the still waters (Psalm 23)!

THE MAIN CULPRIT

Because by nature the sheep are easily swayed, most of the answer as to why extremism occurs lies with the leadership. It is a leadership problem. The cause of imbalance is found in the leadership ministries themselves.

If sheep are being hurt by running after extremes it is often the shepherd's fault. Shepherds, teachers and leaders have the responsibility to protect the sheep and to see that nothing harms them. They are accountable according to Scriptures:

"Obey them that have the rule over you, and submit yourselves, for they watch for your souls, as they that must give account..." (Hebrews 13:17).

"My brethren, be not many masters (teachers), knowing that we shall receive

Maintaining
BALANCE
*when winds
of
doctrine
blow*

the greater condemnation (stricter judgment)" James 3:1.

"If the watchman see the sword come, and blow not the trumpet, and the people be not warned; if the sword come, and take any person from among them, he is taken away in his iniquity, but his blood will I require at the watchman's hand" (Ezekiel 33:6).

It is the job of the leaders of the local church to teach and mature the people so that they are not hurt by extremism. The apostles, prophets, pastors, evangelists and teachers were given as a gift by God to the local church to prevent this from happening. When Peter exhorts "to feed" the flock of God, I am convinced that what he had in mind was feeding a "balanced diet" (II Peter 5:2).

CRAFTY ROGUES AND TRICKY MEN

The cause of imbalance is found in the leadership ministries themselves.

But the Apostles of the early church were realistic men, and they knew that not all leaders would take on their responsibility with full integrity. In the Ephesian epistle, Paul said that there was a danger of sheep being carried away "by the sleight of man, and cunning craftiness" (4:14). And in his farewell speech to the Ephesian elders he warned them that some of them were potentially "grievous wolves (savages)" and would enter in and not spare the flock (Acts 20:20).

Paul warned that these false teachers would be from two sources. First, there would be those who were from without of the local church (Acts 20:29). The kind of ministers he referred to would be like those who hold private home meetings and are not accountable to anyone for correction. Also included would be those spectacular religious leaders who openly mock righteousness like Eastern mystic gurus, college professors turned "guru", or those claiming to be divine masters. Then there are preachers and revivalists who visit a church and seduce a following to leave the church and follow after them. In addition there are many charlatans who claim to have discovered some new thing like golden plates, the lost ark, a recipe for an ancient potion, the secrets of a pyramid and the hidden power of crystal consciousness. Many will base a whole system on an obscure scripture verse. Add to these many disgruntled ex-ministers who were disillusioned, or disciplined, and decided to start their own cult or aberrant Christian-style church.

Then secondly, Paul said that men from within the church would arise with doctrines that would take people off into extremes (Acts 20:30, I Corinthians 11:19). This could include pastors who go off on a tangent, as well as someone causing divisions within the congregation.

Whether from within or without, both of these kinds of false teachers are ministers out

Maintaining **BALANCE** *when winds of doctrine blow*

of balance and are not walking worthy of the calling in Christ. They have serious problems with their human nature. They have given in to their carnal, unregenerate natures. They are not being controlled by the Holy Spirit. If you examined each of their lives closely, you would find a serious problem of ignorance or some serious defect in their character. Many have definite character flaws, or personal problems, and in the final analysis that is the root cause of extremism. That is the ultimate cause of imbalance.

I knew one such man several years ago. He had a very strong and effective ministry. He was the leader of a group in California that also had a lot of influence in Brazil where we had missionaries. He was looked to by many people as an apostle to them. I had received many of his writings and was in agreement with most of what I read. The man had definitely received some insight into the Word of God.

It was not long, however, that problems began to surface in this man's ministry. He began to demand more and more authority in the lives of people until he expected people to treat his words on the same level as God's word. Many people followed him blindly losing the ability to hear from God themselves.

Soon some negative things began to emerge. It seems that behind the scenes this great apostle began an illicit relationship with

If the head is corrupt, the body is soon going to be effected.

another woman. He decided to divorce his wife of many years and marry this younger woman.

In order to be able to do what he wanted to do, he used the authority that he had over the people to convince his followers that what he was doing was the Lord's will for him. It got so bad that the man actually spoke in a prophetic manner using "the voice of the Lord" to confirm his divorce. Those that were under him received this as the word of the Lord and flowed with his decision to divorce.

It was not long before this sickness in the head of this group had its disastrous effect. The man divorced his wife, took the other woman and justified his actions as God's will. Soon all of the churches over which this man had influence were experiencing a wave of immorality and divorce. Many broken homes were left in the wake. If the head is corrupt, the body is soon going to be effected. Fortunately, the Lord took this man off the scene through death before he could do any more damage. If your personal life is not in order, it will effect your teaching.

GIVEN TO FEAR

A predominate trait that you will often find in a leader who leads people to extremes is the spirit of fear. This person is given to fear, his teachings are based on fear, and he

Maintaining **BALANCE** *when winds of doctrine blow*

plays upon fears of the people. This subtle character flaw will pave the way for an imbalance to come into the Church of Jesus Christ.

Some of the prophetic warnings concerning end time events could lead the casual or uninformed reader to become fearful. But when we understand God's commitment to His people we never need to be guided by or even give place to fear. The Holy Spirit warns local churches during persecution, during the fall of nations, and during the end times, but never to bring fear. He warns us so we will roll up our sleeves, go to work and bring in the harvest, or to save the harvest from the impending storm. His warning is not a signal for us to hide under the bed and tremble because of what is coming. It is not designed to get us to sell what we have and run to the wilderness so evil will not find us. It should not inspire us to go start a private, secluded commune so we remain untainted by the evil in the world. Some churches have done these things and as a result they have gone into extreme.

There are some scriptures that could be construed as "gloomy". But if you only read the "gloomy" scriptures you are going to live in fear and not in peace.

His warning is not a signal for us to hide under the bed and tremble

"These things I have spoken unto you, that in me ye might have peace. In the world ye shall have tribulation, but be of

good cheer! I have overcome the world"
(John 16:33).

Light shines best in darkness. Darkness does not put out light. On the contrary, light makes darkness flee! When things appear to be gloomy, that is the time for the church to arise and shine. Speaking of this age, the prophet said:

"Arise, shine; for thy light is come, and the glory of the Lord is risen upon thee. For behold, the darkness shall cover the earth, and gross darkness the people; but the LORD shall arise upon thee, and His glory shall be seen upon thee. And the Gentiles shall come to thy light, and kings to the brightness of thy rising" (Isaiah 60:1-3).

God wants the church to arise, not out of fear so they can run and hide, but because there are multitudes sitting in darkness who need to see the light. In the New Testament, the Spirit declared:

"For God hath not given us the spirit of fear, but of power, and of love, and of a sound mind" (II Timothy 1:7).

Maintaining
BALANCE
when winds
of
doctrine
blow

When a leader and his flock are given to fear, it will usually lead to some form of mass paranoia and suspicion. This atmosphere will give birth to all kinds of irrational action and imbalance.

PERVERTED DESIRES

A minister with perverted desires is one who has a character flaw that will sooner or later lead to imbalance and deception. This person is given to carnal desires. He begins teaching a new morality which caters to the lusts and baser nature in his flock.

The Apostle Peter spends a great deal of time describing the corrupt nature of this kind of false teacher:

> "...them that walk after the flesh in the lust of uncleanness...having eyes full of adultery, and that cannot cease from sin, beguiling unstable souls; an heart they have exercised with covetous practices; cursed children" (II Peter 2:10, 14, see vs.18-22, and Jude 16-19).

There was a man whom I met many years ago who had a very large work on the West Coast. He was a loner and was looking for fellowship. I personally reached out to him to try to develop some kind of friendship, but there was a spirit of pride about him because of his success that caused him to close in. He put up walls and would not reach out to have a close relationship with anybody else. His church was several thousand in attendance, but he was isolated in his own world.

As time went on, this man, who started out right, got into some extreme teaching on "soul mating." He believed that the person that

No one should isolate themselves

you were married to was not necessarily the one that the Lord had put in your life as a mate for life as well as the life to come, and that the Lord would show you the true spiritual soul mating that was to take place. Many of the couples soon began to look beyond their marriage partners for their "soul mate." The result of this perverted teaching was that all moral restraint was removed from the church and divorces began to be a common occurrence. This once great church was led into chaos as the media picked up this perverted teaching and it became a national reproach to the work of God. No one should isolate themselves to the place that other churches and church leaders do not have the influence and are not able to speak into their life.

There are many congregations and groups who have gone astray following after this type of individual. Leaders of this sort use craftiness and beguiling speech to remove the guilt feelings, take away the moral inhibitions, and desensitize the people so they no longer blush at sin and sinful pursuits (Jeremiah 6:15,; 8:12).

No one starts out in their ministry in this condition. These tendencies usually start small but if they remain unchecked they will gradually increase. When these tendencies and lustful desires are given in to they keep demanding more and more expression to remain satisfied. One thing easily leads to another.

Maintaining **BALANCE** *when winds of doctrine blow*

The tragic story of King David is a classic example. Just giving in to one look led to scheming, murder, and a curse on his whole household. Then it continued with the gross lust of Solomon and his thousand wives and concubines! From this flaw in leadership concupiscence broke forth into the vast unrestrained corruption of all Judah including its priests, prophets, princes and people.

"I have seen thine adulteries, and thy neighings, the lewdness of thy whoredom, and thine abominations on the hills in the fields. Woe unto thee, O Jerusalem! Wilt thou not be made clean?" (Jeremiah 13:27, 23:14).

A minister who ignores the wisdom of Proverbs concerning the strange woman (Proverbs 4 and 5) is going to ruin his own life, destroy families, and unleash a plague that will destroy many lives.

WEAK CONVICTIONS

We need to make sure that the things we are involved in are proven.

A man of weak convictions is not going to provide stability in a church, and his leadership will often produce imbalance. A leader must have strong determination and fortitude. He has to have the ability to confront and test all new teachings. Unproven doctrines, untested fads, and novel practices can reek havoc in a congregation.

"I besought thee to abide still at Ephesus...that thou mightest <u>charge</u> some that they teach no other doctrine, neither give heed to fables and endless genealogies, which minister questions, rather than godly edifying..." (I Timothy 1:3-4).

"These things speak, and exhort, and <u>rebuke with all authority</u>. Let no man despise thee...these things I will that thou affirm constantly....A man that is an heretic after the first and second admonition <u>reject</u>, knowing that he that is such is subverted, and sinneth, being condemned of himself" (Titus 2:15, 3:8, 10-11).

"<u>Prove</u> all things; hold fast that which is good" (I Thessalonians 5:21).

We need to make sure that the things we are involved in are proven. A man who is weak or negligent in this area is going to have a flock going off from one extreme to another.

When I first started pastoring some people in our church were involved with a small group that seemed "real spiritual." Because I did not know any better I let it carry on in our church. Soon, however, it was out of control, way off base, and it influenced about a third of our church, including some very influential families.

A lady who was taken up with this super spiritual, deeper life, "know-more-than-anyone-else" clique approached me one day and said

Maintaining
BALANCE
when winds of doctrine blow

she had a word from God for me. "Don't be concerned with what is going on; it will all be okay" she said.

This group had been meeting for a year or so, and I had honestly been a little uneasy about it. However, when she made this statement to me something clicked. I said, "Sister, that's God's word for you. Don't get involved. But I am the shepherd, I'm going to get involved."

I had been praying off in a corner that the problem would all go away. But I suddenly realized that was not why God had put shepherds in the body. Shepherds are suppose to go out and confront the wolves. It took the words of this woman to stir up in me an understanding of my responsibility.

We need to make sure that if there is something wrong or questionable going on in the House of God, we are not neglecting to check it out. And when you do, if you do not approve of what is going on or if those who are involved have a spirit about them that is contrary to the Spirit of Christ, then do not let them function and persist in what they are doing.

Shepherds are suppose to go out and confront the wolves.

"Beloved, believe not every spirit, but try the spirits whether they are of God; because many false prophets are gone out into the world" (I John 4:1).

PRIDE

Pride in a spiritual leader is a sure sign of impending doom. Pride has a way of backing a man into a corner from which there is no escape.

"If any man teach otherwise and consent not to wholesome words, even the words of our Lord Jesus Christ, and to the doctrine which is according to godliness, he is <u>proud</u>, knowing nothing, but doting about questions and strifes of words, whereof cometh envy, strife, railings, evil surmisings, perverse disputings of men of corrupt minds, and destitute of the truth..." (I Timothy 6:3-5).

Pride says "We have all the answers. We don't need help. We don't need outside counsel. No one else has what we have." This reflects a deep spirit of pride. And the Lord says He knows the proud afar off (Psalm 138:6). In fact, God resists the proud (James 4:6, I Peter 5:5). He resists the proud to the degree that the Bible says that He will destroy the house of the proud (Proverbs 15:25), and He scatters the proud in the imagination of their hearts (Luke 1:51). It is a tragedy today that many of God's people are scattered all over the country. Much of this has happened because of proud leaders who have been judged by God.

Maintaining
BALANCE
*when winds
of
doctrine
blow*

"Knowledge puffeth up, but charity edifieth. And if any man think that he knoweth anything, he knoweth nothing yet as he ought to know" (I Corinthians 8:1).

If a teacher of doctrine comes to any of our churches, refuses to submit his doctrine to scrutiny, and refuses to be corrected, watch out. If you do not deal with it immediately it is going to lead to problems that will eventually destroy your church. Pride will cause a person to hold on to a doctrine and refuse to change even when that doctrine is wrong, or is being stretched to unscriptural extremes. Pride blinds that person to the truth and the need for balance in his ministry. Pride over estimates one's own abilities and conclusions.

A young man that grew up in our church and was a spiritual son to me had this root of pride. I saw this as he was growing up and prayed for him often that he would be able to overcome it. As he was being trained I saw a critical spirit that would lead him to challenge every teacher in some area of their teaching. He might agree with ninety-nine percent of what was said, but somehow he felt that he must challenge the one percent.

Pride has a way of backing a man into a corner

There is nothing wrong with challenging your teachers when done in the right spirit. We all have minor areas about which we do not totally agree. But the spirit in this young man was of such a nature that his view became the only right view. Although this young man was able to temper the manifestation of his pride for the sake of peace it was never really dealt with.

This young man was later sent out and started a church under our covering. In the first few years the church grew to an influential church in its community. The number of people in attendance grew to several hundred, but under the surface this pride was still there. From time to time, since we were the sending church, people would call and complain about his hard handed rule and his inflexibility in his leadership style.

When these calls would come I would try to help him see things from a different point of view but that same argumentative spirit was always present. It was always very difficult to adjust him in his attitudes. His view of things was always the correct view.

Maintaining **BALANCE** *when winds of doctrine blow*

As time went on this pastor was influenced heavily by a teaching that was quite different from what had been established in the church he had founded. These teachings were contrary to the direction that he had taken the church up to that time. When he decided that these teachings were true he quickly ran to implement changes in the church without counsel and without regard for the beliefs of the people that he himself had taught.

The people could not take the rapid change of direction. They were choked with the word that was now coming to them and they had a hard time digesting it. Inspite of this the pastor continued to press forward. People started to withdraw and soon a church of several hundred dwindled to less than a hundred and finally dissolved under his leadership. Someone else took the church over but pride kept this man from humbling himself and admitting that he was wrong. His pride caused him to destroy a great church.

Pride is the root of all sin. Doctrinal and spiritual pride will easily lead you into extremes, especially when you cannot be adjusted. You can be so proud that even though you err, pride will not let you admit it.

COVETOUSNESS

In the second epistle of Peter where Peter dealt with the subject of false teachers, he listed a character flaw that is most pervasive among them:

They forsake the example of Moses who forsook the riches of Egypt

"...there shall be false teachers among you...and through <u>covetousness</u> shall they with feigned words make merchandise of you...which have forsaken the right way, and are gone astray, following the way of Balaam, the son of Bosor, who loved the <u>wages</u> of unrighteousness..." (II Peter 2:1, 3, 15, Jude 11).

The small spark of greed, avarice, or covetousness can explode like a small match fire in a dry forest and it can soon bring imbalance and destruction to a church. Covetousness can so infect leadership that it pushes the true emphasis of the Gospel far into the background, and the only real focus that can be seen is the desire for monetary success and prosperity. Soon fiscal corruption sets in. The self-sacrificing aspect of the ministry is quickly lost (II Corinthians 6:10, I Corinthians 4:11, Acts 3:6). These "big time" ministers would be out of place with Peter who said to the lame man, "Silver and gold have I none, but such as I have give I thee!"

They follow in the tradition of the corrupt Israelites of the late monarchies who were described by the prophets:

> *"The heads thereof judge for reward, and the priests thereof teach for hire, and the prophets thereof divine for money..."*
> *(Micah 3:11).*

They forsake the example of Moses who forsook the riches of Egypt (Hebrews 11:24-26), and who only appointed and delegated elders who were "men of truth, hating covetousness" (Exodus 18:21).

They have not heeded the wise example of Daniel who turned down reward from Belshazzar (Daniel 5:17), Elisha who refused commensuration from the healed, leprous Naaman (II Kings 5:16), and Peter who refused

Maintaining
BALANCE
when winds
of
doctrine
blow

money from the sorcerer (Acts 8:20).

Nor do they follow the advice of Jesus Christ who placed a great emphasis on being aware of the dangers of covetousness:

"Take heed, and beware of covetousness; for a man's life consisteth not in the abundance of the things which he possesseth" (Luke 12:15).

"Ye cannot serve God and mammon" (Matthew 6:24).

Instead they stumble along the same path of Judas who sold Jesus for money (Matthew 26:15).

"The love of money is the root of all evil" and if you want a congregation to go into extremism and be destroyed, one of the fastest ways is for a leader, given to greed, to start catering to the base desires of human nature for wealth and fortune (I Timothy 6:10, James 5:3).

A young evangelist once came to our church back when I first started pastoring. After the various meetings I noticed that he took every opportunity to talk to the elderly ladies in the congregation. At first, I thought it was great that he would pay so much attention to the elderly. But then I became suspicious.

Sure enough. One of these ladies had just

Covetousness destroys lives and ruins ministries

come into a large amount of money. She had sold some property to an oil company and had gotten thousands of dollars. A huge amount!

One day she came to me and announced that she was leaving the church to go with this young evangelist to buy a boat and sail the Caribbean to preach to the natives! Immediately I could see that she was just being manipulated and being "made merchandise of." Though I pleaded and begged and warned her to stay and keep her money, she left.

It wasn't but a short time that she came back, penniless! She was not only penniless, but also disillusioned, embittered and despondent. I do not know to this day if she ever got over being angry at the evangelist, the church, the world, and at God. That is sad.

Covetousness not only destroys lives and ruins ministries, but it brings scandal and open reproach upon the Gospel. We are not to let covetousness even be named among us as leaders. It has to be totally eradicated (Ephesians 5:3, Colossians 3:5).

CLOSED-MINDEDNESS

Another trait in an overseer that will cause him to fall prey to extremes and imbalance is closed-mindedness or a lack of objectivity. This kind of leader sees only one side of a truth, and then runs with it. He has an incomplete vision.

Maintaining **BALANCE** *when winds of doctrine blow*

I remember a story that I heard once of blind men trying to describe an elephant from India. One blind man felt the trunk and said "an elephant is like a tree." Another man felt the long tail and testified "an elephant is like a rope." Still another felt the side of the elephant and proclaimed "an elephant is like a wall." Obviously all of those blind men were right in a limited sense but they did not have a complete picture.

A quick way to have imbalance is to lack complete vision and to focus on only one aspect of truth without seeking a complete, broad understanding on a particular subject. We could easily end up like those men who were describing the elephant. It does not mean that you are wrong in that particular facet of truth upon which you are focusing, but you simply do not have the complete picture. When you are able to see the more complete picture you will be able to balance your insight, truth, or revelation with the larger body of revelation provided in God's word.

That is why a person's ministerial education and training needs to be well-rounded. A life that is only ministered to by a singular aspect of truth will be out of balance. Experiencing life from different viewpoints provides an understanding and perspective that will bring stability and will increase a person's humility and tolerance toward other viewpoints.

I understand this from my own experience. I grew up in a church group that focused

A life that is only ministered to by a singular aspect of truth will be out of balance.

exclusively on the deliverance ministry. As a result, when my father and I pastored we called our church "Deliverance Temple." And as you can imagine, we built the church around one emphasis--deliverance. The name of a church will often give you a key to the particular emphasis of that church. This was certainly true in our case.

As we progressed in our leadership we were wondering why our congregation was not stable. We kept cycling and recycling people. They would come in the front door and soon leave out the back door. We were having tremendous meetings with many people getting healed and delivered from great bondage and entrenched habit patterns. We prayed for the sick constantly because that was our main message. Healing and deliverance was "the name of the game", and that was it! And we did that for fifteen years.

We were like a specialty restaurant. We were like a taco house, a pancake house, a steak house, or a hamburger stand. Some might consider this ministry a "milk" ministry, but I viewed it as strong meat or the "steak house" ministry. Please understand me, it is a good message. But, how many can really enjoy steak three times a day, every single day? No one! We all like it occasionally, and we all need it occasionally, but not all the time! Truthfully, if that is all you eat it will be harmful to your body.

Maintaining
BALANCE
when winds
of
doctrine
blow

Our lives had been touched by one aspect of church doctrine. But God had to deal with us about our narrow vision and closed mindedness. One of the first things we did was change our name. Our church is now called "Bible Temple." And we endeavor to preach the "whole counsel of God."

INSECURITY

Insecurity is a subtle characteristic of human nature that many do not realize can cause imbalance. Some ministers and churches feel inadequate or insecure in their ministry, and to make up for it they seek out a unique identity.

This happens with adolescents all the time. They are uncertain about who they are, they are insecure about their future, and they are wondering just where they fit in.

So one day they decide to identify with a certain hero. After a short time they have given up that hero and start imitating someone else, perhaps a famous singer. And the next week they are following yet another person or group.

Sometimes an adolescent will so identify with a certain group or group leader that it becomes his all-consuming passion. He dresses like them, talks like them and walks like them. During this time he usually pays very little

Many do not realize insecurity can cause imbalance.

attention to other areas of his life that need developing, such as job skills, communication skills, social needs, hygiene and grooming.

This type of thing can also happen with churches. They can manufacture a new identity by over-emphasizing a particular doctrine and let it become their all-consuming passion. Or they can join a movement that happens to be sweeping across their area at that particular time, which is emphasizing a certain doctrine. Soon other areas of church life become neglected. The local church then becomes imbalanced.

All of this has taken place in their experience because of insecurity. They looked at these growing movements with envy and, because they did not have an inner confidence in the unique thing that God wanted to do in and through them, they reached for something else which had the outward trappings of success. In doing so they lost their balance, problems arose and soon they reached toward another "success" ministry for their answer. Churches that fall into this category can make very wide swings from imbalance to imbalance.

IMPATIENCE

When the unregenerate or carnal nature sees something it likes, it usually wants it "now." The culture in which we live, with all of its commercial advertising, really caters to

Maintaining
BALANCE
when winds
of
doctrine
blow

this nature. Companies advertise instant potatoes, instant weight loss, instant success, instant coffee, instant pudding (which makes the instant weight loss necessary), and even instant T.V. dinners.

This type of a mentality can be a real trap in church life. Ministers often get fed up with immature sheep, and if you have pastored long enough you know that some sheep have a hard time of ever maturing! We get very tired of the imperfections we see in certain members of our congregation. We want to see them mature instantly. So some pastors will start teaching the deliverance ministry to an extreme, thinking that all we need to do is cast out the demons of imperfection like jealousy, anger, bitterness and hate. Got a problem? Just cast it out with one prayer! Wouldn't it be wonderful if it was that easy.

I want you to hear me carefully here. I am not belittling deliverance. But Christian maturity is a growth process, and growth takes time. God has ways of working out our imperfections. It takes many unique experiences, various tribulations and much processing to build godly character.

Growth takes time.

We short change people if we promise them that a particular practice or doctrine will be an instant "cure-all" for them. Whether this "cure-all" is a new water baptism that we promise will provide instant sanctification; or deliverance that will instantly solve all of their problems; or the giving of money that will insure instant blessing in return; or even that repentance unto salvation will bring quick happiness and a trouble-free style; all of these can lead to frustration and imbalance.

Growth takes time. We must adjust our thinking to that of God's who has "long patience" waiting for the precious fruit of the earth.

FRUSTRATED SPIRIT

A frustrated spirit, especially one that is caused by a lack of ministerial success, also causes some to enter the realm of imbalance. Because these pastors are not doing well, their frustration puts them into a vulnerable position where they can be tempted to resort to extreme measures, outlandish teachings and questionable programs.

For example, one of the popular emphases is in the area of church growth. And if church growth is not happening in your own church, a pastor can be easily tempted to try novel things to attract new members. The pressure to keep up with other churches pushes them into doing things they would not ordinarily do or teach. They may grasp at straws, anything to make growth happen and establish their credibility as a viable ministry.

Church growth is a vital doctrine. It is important. But it is only one aspect or facet of the whole. It is not sufficient reason to forsake balance just to keep up with the

Maintaining **BALANCE** *when winds of doctrine blow*

proverbial "Jones'." And this same principle is true with any other doctrine. Any doctrine, no matter how helpful or wonderful, cannot be preached at the expense or exclusion of other aspects of truth.

PRAYERLESSNESS

A life not characterized by prayer will inevitably go off into some form of extremism. A person in leadership simply cannot be involved in the ministry, which is a spiritual task, without having spiritual power. You can not expect to have power over the forces of darkness by simply having a form of religiosity without the spiritual power to back it up. The seven sons of Sceva learned this the hard way (Acts 19:13-16).

Leadership ministry is spiritual in nature. It has to face the challenge of spiritual principalities, powers, and wickedness in high (extremely high) places (II Corinthians 10:4).

"Put on the whole armor of God, that ye may be able to stand against the wiles of the devil. [First warning!]

For we wrestle not against flesh and blood, but against principalities, against powers, against the rulers of the darkness of this world, against spiritual wickedness in high places.

Wherefore take unto you the whole armor of God, that ye may be able to withstand

Leadership ministry is spiritual in nature.

*in the evil day, and having done all to
stand... [Second warning!]*

*[By means of] praying with all prayer and
supplication in the Spirit, and watching
thereunto with all perseverance and
supplication for all saints..."* *(Ephesians
6:11-13,18).*

For this reason leaders and their congregations
must be adequately equipped. The only way
for a leader to be so equipped is by means of
prayer. The fighting is too fierce, the warfare

too treacherous, the enemy too subtle, the
tactics too complex, and the consequences too
severe to try to go it alone. You have got to
stay next to the side of Jesus in order to make
it.

An independent spirit, an attitude of self-
sufficiency, are lethal to any ministry. If
leaders do not watch and pray, they <u>will</u> fall
into temptation (Matthew 26:41)! Satan will
be able to lead pastors and church leaders into
all sorts of extremes and deception unless they
maintain a close communion with God.

Maintaining
BALANCE
*when winds
of
doctrine
blow*

The daily prayer of every pastor should be
that he would not be led into temptation in his
own personal life and especially in the carrying
out of his responsibility of teaching and leading
the congregation (Luke 11:4).

PERSONAL INVENTORY

If we were to take an inventory of the personalities of each of the notorious leaders who have caused congregations to shipwreck, I am quite sure that at least one of these negative traits would be clearly seen. We would find leaders who are given to fear, wrongful desires, weak convictions, pride, covetousness, closed mindedness, insecurity, impatience, frustration of spirit, prayerlessness and a lack of compassion. These traits, when not dealt with, have the potential of "leavening the whole lump."

However, the fact that these things exist and the negative impact that they can have should cause us to re-examine our own lives with a spiritual thermometer. They should be an incentive for us to judge ourselves (Romans 14:10-13, I Corinthians 11:28, II Corinthians 13:5). Once we have examined ourselves we should ask God to help us deal with any of these tendencies that might be in us so that we do not lead the people of God on the road to imbalance.

"Search me, O God, and know my heart; try me, and know my thoughts; and see if there be any wicked way in me, and lead me in the way everlasting" (Psalm 139:23-24).

If leaders do not watch and pray, they will fall into temptation

"...my son, know thou the God of thy father, and serve Him with a perfect heart and with a willing mind; for the LORD searcheth all hearts, and understandeth all the imaginations of the thoughts; if thou seek Him, he will be found of thee; but if thou forsake Him, He will cast thee off forever. Take heed now; for the LORD hath chosen thee to build an house for the sanctuary; be strong and do it" (I Chronicles 28:9-10).

Maintaining
BALANCE
when winds
of
doctrine
blow

TWO

CONSEQUENCES OF IMBALANCE

A person does not have to work with many churches in upheaval before he begins to see the sad consequences of doctrinal extreme and of imbalance. I have been called on by many of these hurting churches and have had the unenviable job of trying to put back together the remaining pieces.

LOSS OF CONFIDENCE IN LEADERSHIP

When the leadership allows or even promotes a running after every "wind of doctrine," people lose confidence in the ability of the leadership. If a church leadership tells the people that a teaching or a particular program is the "answer", then the next year "the answer" is something else, the people begin to wonder. "What ever happened to last year's program?" "I thought you said..." "How do we know this new emphasis isn't going to be replaced too?"

Maintaining **BALANCE** *when winds of doctrine blow*

It is a sad thing when people lose confidence in their leadership. It is easy for people who are in this condition to start going off on their own. Instead of following the shepherd, they follow their own "leading" and end up being scattered all over the hillside. Then the wolves show up and take advantage of these sheep.

I met a teacher many years ago who got caught up in what I call "survival mentality." This man was so extreme in his teaching that he believed that there was a group of people that the Lord was going to take "out into the wilderness" and preserve them and that he and his following were chosen by God to be that "elect" company. He had a number of survival camps in different countries.

I met some people who went into one of these survival camps in South America. They isolated themselves in the jungle and were going to have their own society. The only problem was that in that type of isolation they became very agitated with each other and finally they found themselves fighting among themselves. The end result is they lost their desire to serve the Lord and lost faith in those who directed the work of God that they were under. Many of them, to this day, have never really returned to the church but are backslidden and full of resentment.

Wrong teaching will eventually destroy the spirit of faith from which many will never

Wrong teaching will eventually destroy the spirit of faith.

recover. No one should be allowed to take a group of people and isolate them by their teaching from the rest of the body of Christ. Whatever the Lord is saying He is going to say it simultaneously across the whole earth. America does not have a corner on God.

Many years ago there was a great church in our area in which there was a genuine move of the Holy Spirit. This body of believers was touched mightily by the Lord. The leader developed a very large and influential radio ministry. In that day, the radio was the main source of communication nationally. This gave him a very costly budget to maintain every month to support the national ministry.

The problem that gradually developed was that as the move of the Holy Spirit subsided from its dramatic earlier days, the finances began to drop and he was not willing to adjust his ministry according to the changed spiritual climate. He began to approach this problem not by cutting back, but by gimmicks and quackery that would excite the people to give to his cause. His church began to promote the latest gimmicks and crowd pleasers to support the work. It was not long before the people got tired of the gimmicks and the church itself became a scandal in the community. In addition, the man soon lost his local church and his national ministry and had to live in reproach because the people no longer had confidence in his leadership.

Maintaining **BALANCE** *when winds of doctrine blow*

Whenever you try to promote the cause of Christ with gimmicks, you might as well shut your door because the end is coming very quickly and the people will see through it eventually. It may create excitement for a short season, but it is the beginning of the end for that work.

LOSS OF THE SPIRIT OF FAITH

When people have given themselves to the teachings of their leadership and those teachings and programs do not produce the fruit that was promised, the people become disheartened and end up losing the spirit of faith. This is tragic. Leaders must not do anything that would cause the congregation to lose faith, because faith is your motivating force. The just live by faith. Too many side-trips, too many involvements in tributaries, too many disappointments will rob the people of God of the drive and the motivation to carry on the vision of the house of God.

I know of a man who had an excellent ministry, but he got out of balance through a teaching on "cleansing." He felt that in order for us to be really true worshipers of God, we had to "cleanse" our spirit, our minds, our hands, our walk, before we could enter into the holy hill of God. When he came into churches with this message and called on the people to "cleanse" themselves, there seemed to be an initial response. He would preach for

The just live by faith.

an hour or more on how unworthy we are to come before a holy God, how our minds are polluted with evil thoughts and attitudes, and that we have no right to come before the Lord with such evil in our heart. He taught that all of us are guilty of these evil thoughts and attitudes every week and even every day.

After this man would preach an hour or more in this condemnatory style, the people were encouraged to literally prostrate themselves before the Lord and say in their spirit, heart, and with their lips, "how unworthy of a worm I am." So the congregation all laid on the floor and there they "repented" of the filth they had in them.

The response to this emotional appeal was evidenced by much tears, weeping and mourning. After a season of this, then the people were told that they could stand and enter into sanctified worship to the Lord. After many tears, and this psychological release that they had experienced, called "cleansing," they were now to have a liberty they had never experienced in their worship.

The only problem was, every service had to go this way. This was not a one time act, but this was a routine. What it produced was heaviness over the congregation and a loss of the personal righteousness that comes through Christ whereby we stand in faith. It took away the peace and the joy of the congregation.

Maintaining
BALANCE
when winds
of
doctrine
blow

Every pastor that I have met from churches that practiced this man's teaching for any length of time told me that the thing they noticed was the spirit of joy departed and a heavy cloud of condemnation came upon the congregation. Whenever you loose the spirit of faith and you give yourself to these erroneous teachings, there will be no positive fruit that will last.

EXTRA STRESS

When a church moves into a place of imbalance there is going to be much more stress on the pastor of that church than on other ministers. It is just like a car when one of the wheels is out of balance. The faster you go the more stress it puts on the rest of the car. Before long the front end goes out. And if this situation is not corrected the car is going to end up in the ditch.

When the church is out of balance, problems in the pastor's life increase. Because he is not staying within the "stream of God," the river of God in a church soon overflows its banks, starts cutting off into another channel, or spills into flood lands. Soon the pastor has to run around and try to minimize the damage, appease people, make sure families are not leaving, and solve many other related problems. Often pastors will spend many anxious nights lying awake thinking of rational justification to give to the people to explain the years that

When the church is out of balance, problems in the pastor's life increase.

were lost in the last tributary and why the revelation he is sharing today is the "real" truth.

EMBITTERED FEELINGS

Many people who show up at our churches have come out of situations where there was tremendous confusion and disillusionment. They walk in through our doors hurt and embittered.

Some victims cannot even make it back into a good church! They have given up. "I've tried it. I gave my life savings. I gave my all. I sold my house and ran after this modern movement which was teaching a particular 'truth,' and it all blew up!" They are so disillusioned by the extremes and false emphases that they do not even now want to follow that which is the truth. They have lost their ability to trust and they are not sure whether they want to commit themselves to anyone or any body of believers. They fear that they may be let down once again.

LOSS OF INFLUENCE

A church that is known for its fanaticism or its wavering will soon lose its influence. Not only will it lose its influence in the church world, but it will lose its power to influence the community as well. When a church brings reproach to the Gospel of Christ by its actions

Maintaining **BALANCE** *when winds of doctrine blow*

and doctrines, it is a double disaster. The involved congregation is one victim. But another victim is the unsaved individual who needed the church to be a lighthouse to guide them in their lives. They find no help from such a church and must go looking somewhere else. They turn to other religions, drugs, or other influences. The occasion of reproach has, in effect, built up a barrier between the lost world and the local church.

IMMATURITY

Many times when we move into some area of emphasis there is a temporary excitement, a temporary enthusiasm. This new focus may give a local church a spiritual "shot in the arm." Everyone gets excited about this new direction, new movement, or new truth. It has a tremendous initial impact. But if it is not quickly brought into balance and integrated with the body of established truth, it will soon lose its impact and the excitement wanes.

A church that is known for its fanaticism will soon lose its influence.

I used to be interested in the "two week" revival. These special meetings were a great way to get the people all excited. After many years of experience, however, I am not nearly so interested in them. I found that they served a great function to get people stirred up for a month or two, but as soon as the evangelist left town, it seemed that he took the "revival" with him. It was not long before people were back to where they had been before the revival and we had to believe God to send us another evangelist. It became a vicious cycle.

The thing that I am most interested in now as a pastor is in long term, consistent, on-going growth, change and maturity in the people of God. I am not simply interested in spurts of excitement, short term conversions or continual rededications. I am interested in consistent, continual growth for my congregation in their Christian walk. Maturity is a steady process. If we maintain a positive balance there is much more chance that maturity will take place. Maturity will never come by "chasing the wind."

DIVISION IN THE BODY

Churches that go to the extremes in a particular doctrine open the door to division in the Body of Christ. Often times people are forced to take sides on the issues that are being taught. The unfortunate natural consequence of this is church members find themselves taking stands against other church members, local churches begin taking stands against other local churches, and even denominations can begin slandering denominations.

This situation must grieve the Spirit of God who desires and is unceasingly working toward the unity of the Body of Christ. The Spirit was given to bring us to the same mind, the mind of Christ. Truth taken to extreme

Maintaining **BALANCE** *when winds of doctrine blow*

and promoted at the expense of other important truths can do nothing but divide.

MOVEMENT TOWARD DECEPTION

Over-emphasizing a doctrine to the extreme can, in a lot of cases, lead to a more serious condition which is deception. Often the process is so gradual it can hardly be noticed. The person sitting next to you in church is your friend; the book read every Sunday is the Bible; and the man preaching is your shepherd. A person sitting in the pew just does not suspect deception is going to occur, or may have already occurred.

No one ever enters into deception intentionally. No one who is truly deceived is even aware of the fact that they are. Deception involves the believing of a lie. The lie in this case is subtle because in many cases it is based on the truth. But truth taken to an extreme is heresy. And in this case it can be just as damaging as error.

DISTORTED JUDGMENT

No one ever enters into deception intentionally.

When there is imbalance there is a development of distorted judgment. People develop a distorted perspective. They lose their ability to look at things objectively. And they often make irrational decisions that affect their lives and their future. Caught up in the excitement, the dogmatism, or in the induced fear, they often get themselves into serious trouble by making bad decisions.

Every once in a while you will hear about a group of people who have gone to an extreme in the area of "healing." We all believe in the power of God to heal and yet that does not mean that it is wrong or a lack of faith to seek the help of a doctor. At times you will hear of a child who has died because the parents refused medical assistance. Because of an extreme view on healing these people were not able to exercise common sense when their child was in serious condition. You cannot see things clearly when you take an extreme posture. Your judgment can easily become clouded.

FORTRESS MENTALITY

One of the most dangerous consequences of extremism is the tendency to become defensive. Dogmatism often leads to sectarianism, exclusiveness, and in some cases a fearful paranoia, where those involved start defending their position in irrational ways. At times they may even resort to physical violence to defend their narrow-minded position or to advance their beliefs. It is not uncommon to read in the newspapers of some extremist religious group that is stock-piling weapons.

Maintaining **BALANCE** *when winds of doctrine blow*

When you try to talk with members of an extreme group you will see them put up their defenses immediately. Their attitude is evident in their demeanor. They have the truth, and everyone else is wrong and an enemy. No one can be trusted. This is tragic. But it is a consequence of extremism.

These consequences of imbalance should motivate us to do everything that we can to maintain ourselves in a balanced position so that we can truly lead people into green pastures and beside still waters.

Our goal as pastors is to bring people to maturity and to equip them for a balanced ministry. If people lose confidence in their leaders, if they lose faith in God, if they become burned out by stress, if they become bitter, divided or deceived, they will never be able to accomplish God's will for their lives.

God help us to maintain Godly balance in all areas for the sake of His precious people.

You cannot see things clearly when you take an extreme posture.

THREE

HOW TO MAINTAIN BALANCE

On the day of Pentecost the Jews, who had just killed the Messiah fifty days prior, realized they were in dire straits. Their lives had been governed so much by a fanatical zeal for the letter of the Law that nearly all of Israel had gone to an extreme. They were so out of balance with religious teaching and conduct that they had beaten and killed one who was now exalted as Lord. The one they had mistreated was now in charge! They were now in a precarious position (Acts 2:33-36)!

Being out of balance in doctrinal areas puts us all in a precarious position. The Jews responded to their predicament by asking, "Men and brethren, what shall we do?" Perhaps it would be good for all of us to ask that same question, especially if we have been driven by the winds of imbalance.

It might even be wiser if we, for the sake of preventing problems, asked instead, "Men and brethren, what can we do to prevent

Maintaining **BALANCE** *when winds of doctrine blow*

imbalance from occurring at all? How can we maintain balance in our local churches?"

There are nine principles that I have learned over the years that have always helped me whenever I have been tempted to go after a good sounding doctrine. These principles are very practical and I believe they will work for everyone.

STICK TO CLEAR SCRIPTURES

If the churches of today are going to maintain balance, the leaders of those churches must maintain balance. One of the ways that a leader maintains doctrinal balance is in his approach to the Word of God.

When a leader goes to the Word of God for doctrinal understanding, he must focus on the plain, clear verses. Leaders must avoid running to some obscure verses that theologians have been arguing over for centuries because of their vagueness. Do not focus your vision, for example, on some vague prophetic scripture in an allegoric setting with symbols and signs, and try to establish a major doctrine or emphasis. You are heading for trouble.

Focus on the plain, clear verses.

All of the major teachings of the Bible necessary for the Christian walk are clearly stated. In fact, they are usually stated repeatedly. The principle of "two or three witnesses" applies here (II Corinthians 13:1,

Deuteronomy 19:15). If a teaching is vital to a church you should be able to find it stated clearly several places in the Bible.

I remember one instance where my wife and I were visiting a church. I was to speak that morning. But we didn't happen to be dressed the particular way that that church required. They had a doctrine based on one obscure verse, and they were willing to shut anyone out from fellowship that did not conform to that doctrine! We had to run all over town and find something that would satisfy their code before we could even minister to their congregation.

Any doctrine that is going to be used to prevent ministry or break fellowship should certainly be based on more than just one verse! Too much is at stake to conduct a church in this manner. We have too much to lose when we walk on such thin "theological ice."

The first principle to remember is that if a teaching is worth devoting your life to, and especially worth affecting the Christian community at large, then it is going to be stated repeatedly and clearly in the Bible!

Maintaining **BALANCE** *when winds of doctrine blow*

MAJOR ON THE MAJORS

A church reduces its chances of going off on a tangent if it majors on what the Bible majors on and it minors on what the Bible minors on. We emphasize what God emphasizes! I am not suggesting that we are to ignore the minors, simply that we should not put major emphasis on them.

For example, when Christ spent the last forty days walking on the earth He spoke to His disciples that which was important to Him. That is, the Kingdom of God (Acts 1:3). We should then also place importance on that same topic. We should emphasize the kingdom of God in our preaching.

The Bible places more importance on some subjects than others. When I was an evangelist I placed most of my emphasis on the concept of the universal church. I went from place to place as a traveling minister preaching on how we were all part of the great universal church or the world-wide expression of the Body of Christ. And this is a great doctrine. The "Spirit bears witness that we all are the children of God" no matter if we are English, Japanese, Spanish, or European. That's a great truth.

We emphasize what God emphasizes!

But I have more recently discovered that when the Bible discusses the church, that only ten percent of the time is it dealing with the universal church. Ninety percent of the time it deals with the "local church," that is the local gathering of believers. Up until this time my preaching was not really majoring on what the Bible majored on concerning the church.

As a pastor I always wondered why most churches were not healthy and growing. Then I realized a common mistake. Christians cannot grow in their Christian walk by merely being identified with, related to, and committed to each other as brothers and sisters of some "universal" body. They need to rub shoulders with other Christians in a local gathering. There is no way for a Christian to learn to walk in the concept of unity by only relating to the universal church. For a Christian to develop a spirit of unity, he must be related to specific people in the same house, and look those same people in the face regularly and work out unity with these same people in a practical way.

It is like someone said in a conference seminar that I recently attended, "I have no problem having unity here, I don't have to live with you!" If we do not have to live with each other we can all get along very well! But if we live together in the same flock, there might be some rough edges on fellow saints that rub us the wrong way. This, however, is part of the process of maturity and it is how a lasting unity is going to be developed. We have got to make it work were we live if we want to experience the glory of God. Local church involvement and identification, I have found, is extremely important (II Corinthians 12:12-27).

When we switched our focus and began putting emphasis on the corporate gathering like the New Testament did, our church became more healthy and began to grow. We

Maintaining
BALANCE
when winds
of
doctrine
blow

were now majoring on what the Scriptures majored.

This same principle applies to so many other doctrines as well. Worship is an emphasized doctrine in the Bible. It is not just a fad. From cover to cover, the Bible teaches it strongly. That is why it is being placed in such high regard in more and more churches throughout the world. It is not a sideline. Therefore if we major on worship we are doing just what the Bible does. Majoring on the majors will insure safety and balance.

TEACH THE SHEEP ALERTNESS

To keep your flock, or any part of your flock from running off on a tangent, you must build a protection around them by teaching them about deception and about the existence of "wolves in sheep's clothing." They need to know that Satan comes often as "an angel of light" (II Corinthians 11:14). They need to know the methods, devices and tactics of "false apostles." Our churches will run a lot smoother if the sheep themselves are alert to the dangers of subtle, smooth-talking deceivers. This teaching process will act as a preventative measure.

Members in the congregation need to be equipped to help defend the church from within and without. Sometimes a pastor who

Majoring on the majors will insure safety and balance.

is busy with the thousand and one things associated with pastoring just cannot keep up with everything that is going on in the congregation. So members need to be able to spot those who are leading sheep astray or those who are about to cause division.

Young lambs can be easily swayed by smooth-talking, enticing words and fair speeches (Romans 16:17-18, II Corinthians 11:3). They can be easily deceived by men with tongues smooth as silk who say things like, "Hath God really said...?" "You know there are deeper revelations God is withholding from you until you've arrived at a higher state of awareness." "The elders and pastors here haven't quite arrived, but God is selecting out of the midst of His people a special remnant who have an understanding of a higher illumination. Come and meet with us; we meet every Wednesday. There we share things that can not be shared with anyone except those who have gone on to know the Lord in a deeper way!" And on and on.

People need to be taught that an eloquent person is not always a truthful person. The person who speaks the best is not always the most truthful. Just because a man is a gifted teacher, or talented speaker does not mean his interpretation is the correct one.

Maintaining **BALANCE** *when winds of doctrine blow*

Paul told the Corinthian church that his speech and his preaching "was not with enticing words of man's wisdom..." (II Corinthians 2:4).

In fact, Paul may have been a very poor orator, yet he ministered the truth (II Corinthians 10:10). So the sheep must stay alert and look beyond the words they hear. And as pastors we need to teach them that skill. We need to equip the saints. If members in our church know that the ones doing a lot of "talking" behind the back of the leadership could be deceivers and wolves, they have a better chance of not being deceived by them. They have a much better chance of not being led astray by their false "wind" of doctrine.

WATCH AND PRAY

Another check against imbalance in the church is faithfulness in prayer. Jesus told the disciples to "watch and pray that ye enter not into temptation; the spirit indeed is willing, but the flesh is weak" (Matthew 26:41). We may say, "Oh, I would never get caught up in extremism." Or "Our church would never go off on a tangent and become imbalanced!" Our intentions may be quite sincere. But the flesh is still weak. You just cannot rely upon your own strength.

You just cannot rely upon your own strength.

We all need a supernatural strength to do spiritual warfare, and being a Christian involves spiritual warfare. We need the protection of God's angels daily. Angels are dispatched by God in response to our prayer. God's protecting covering is made further insured when we kneel in humility and acknowledge our dependence upon Him. Our daily prayer should be "deliver us from the evil one" (Luke 11:4).

When it seems that God is revealing a truth to you, or you begin to hear a new sound coming to you through someone else, wait on God. Do not just swallow it and believe every word.   Continue to seek God about it. Patiently inquire about it in prayer. If it is truth, there is no hurry. It will still be there tomorrow. God is not in a panic. He does not have a "last minute" truth that He forgot to tell us about all these centuries.

It is true that sometimes we need to be reminded of truths we have neglected. But they are truths that are already known to the church, that have already been given to the church (II Peter 1:12 "present truth" = truth you already have).   Just as Peter felt it necessary to continually remind his flock of the basics of Christianity, so also there are seasons when the Spirit will emphasize certain truth in our local churches to remind us or so that we do not fall short in any area.

We need to wait on God not only for confirmation of these truths, but also for the wisdom and skill in applying them to the local assembly. We need guidance in handling those truths. We need to pray for receptive ears, soft hearts and willing spirits so the congregation will accept those truths. And we need to pray

Maintaining
BALANCE
when winds
of
doctrine
blow

that no one will take any truth out of balance and end up in an extreme.

Every time King David made a move he preceded his action by "inquiring of the Lord" (II Samuel 2:1, 5:19). And all the other kings that sought God prospered:

"...if thou seek Him, He will be found of thee; but if thou forsake Him, He will cast thee off forever" (I Chronicles 28:9).

"The Lord is with you, while ye be with Him; and if ye seek Him, He will be found of you; but if ye forsake Him, He will forsake you" (II Chronicles 15:2).

"And he (Uzziah) sought God in the days of Zechariah, who had understanding in the visions of God: and as long as he sought the Lord, God made him to prosper" (II Chronicles 26:5).

As leadership in our local churches we too will prosper only when we seek God and wait upon Him. It is the ministry of the Holy Spirit to bear witness of truth. This inner witness will be ours if we maintain a posture of prayer before the Lord.

It is the ministry of the Holy Spirit to bear witness of truth.

CONFER WITH OTHER PASTORS

No one person has total knowledge or understanding of truth. A pastor who draws from a variety of sources in biblical research has a balanced approach to Bible study. The pastor who can see "the other side" of an argument is going to make a more rational decision, most of the time. There is value in another man's opinion, even if it is simply to cause you to "dig deeper" in research or to appreciate the truth you already have. When studying a particular doctrine, we need to consult many sources. The ideas of others will help to put our ideas into perspective (I Corinthians 11:19).

This principle of consultation with others not only applies to research sources, but also to the other ministers within your own local church. It is wonderful when you have a variety of ministering elders, some who are evangelistic, some with a pastoral emphasis, some who are proficient in teaching and some with the prophetic mantle. This provides a valuable system of checks and balances. Any doctrine, practice, or program should be "bounced off" all of them. They all should be continually encouraged to give open and honest input.

Often the apostle and the prophet are mentioned together in the New Testament. I believe that they are paired up in ministry because of their different natures and perspectives. Prophets tend to be lofty and elevated in their spirit and message. They have encouraging, but at times grandiose approaches to difficult times. On the other hand, the

Maintaining
BALANCE
when winds
of
doctrine
blow

apostles seem to be more down to earth and practical in their approach to situations. They make sure things are "set in order" in a very specific way.

Now if a church contained no one but prophets, it does not seem that it would remain balanced for very long. Everyone would be encouraged and lifted in spirit; but not much would be accomplished because there would be little of the organization which is necessary to carry out the great visions. The same would be true with the apostles. A church full of them might easily become bogged down with details unless it had some prophetic ministries to keep the people inspired along the way.

When it comes to keeping balance in our churches it is mandatory that we have a variety of ministries. That is what team ministry is intended to provide.[1] Team ministry provides a means of maintaining doctrinal balance. Team ministers are not meant to be a group of "yes men," but individuals who, in the spirit of humility and love, will honestly and thoughtfully provide an evaluation of matters that arise. That is how team ministry is meant to function.

Team ministry provides a means of maintaining doctrinal balance.

In extending this principle even further, it is also wise to consult with pastors and ministers outside of your own local church. Networking all of our churches together in a spirit of open and honest communication is extremely important. Pastors must spend a certain amount of their time developing and maintaining pastoral relationships both within their local area and on a national and international level. Pastors need to relate to other pastors that they know and trust so that they can discuss and exchange ideas and trends that are stirring Christendom. Pursuing these kind of relationships take time but they will ultimately help to safeguard the local pastor from possible imbalance.

There was a major controversy in doctrine that took place in America during the past decade that ended up causing a lot of problems. One of the leaders of the movement said, "You know, if we had had a forum, a friendly forum where differences could have been discussed, I don't think we would have gotten so far away from where we really wanted to go. But as soon as we started preaching certain things, rocks started coming; and in defense we put up walls. And we just went on and did our thing. We didn't have anyone to speak into our lives that could have brought a balanced perspective." That is sad.

Our local church has started several pioneer churches, so we have a group of churches with which we fellowship. In addition there are hundreds of other pastors that we know with whom we have established a beautiful trust relationship. As a pastor I need to hear what the Spirit is saying both within as well as outside of our fellowship. This becomes even more critical as we see the rise

Maintaining
BALANCE
when winds
of
doctrine
blow

of independent churches. We can not get so independent that we do not hear what others are saying. Together we can keep each other in balance.

If there is no fellowship, no open communication, then all we hear are rumors and gossip. Then suspicion sets in which can easily lead to distrust and accusations.

If, however, there is open fellowship, and we can love each other, then we will be in a position to speak into each other's lives. It does not mean that we agree on each point; but we are able to listen. And that can be a life saver, because when we listen we just might hear something that could prevent us from getting off into extremes. But if there is no forum or no previous relationships established and someone is throwing rocks at you, it becomes very difficult to listen. Their actions speak louder than their words.

It is refreshing when we stop looking at each other over our walls and, instead, sit down together with integrity and an honest desire and seek out what the Lord is doing in the church (Psalm 133).

Pastors need to relate to other pastors

In describing the false apostles and deceivers, Jude said that they "separate themselves" (Jude 19). In other words, they are taken up with an "independent spirit." An independent spirit is a real curse in our day and pastors can be just as guilty as anyone else in this area.

King David got caught up with this spirit of independence once and it cost Israel dearly. He refused the counsel of his fellow leaders (I Chronicles 21:3). On most other occasions David consulted his officers, counselors and advisors on every matter brought forward (I Chronicles 13:1 N.E.B.). That was his safeguard. But when he departed from this principle he failed as the shepherd of Israel.

Leadership sharing counsel with leadership is vital to keeping balance in the church (Proverbs 11:14, 12:15, 15:22). God wants every leader to have a network established of other leaders who can function as their "Ahithophels." It was said of this man in II Samuel 16:23, "And the counsel of Ahithophel, which he counselled in those days, was as if a man had inquired at the oracle of God."

STUDY IT CAREFULLY

Twentieth century American culture has been conditioned to buy commodities on the basis of how cute the commercial jingle is, or how beautiful the wrapper looks, or on the basis of who endorses it. Very seldom are we encouraged to consider the actual merits of the product itself to see if it will produce the desired results.

Maintaining **BALANCE** *when winds of doctrine blow*

Often doctrines are presented to us in the same way. They come in a neat presentation that appeals to our intellectual pride. Or they appeal to the carnal appetites of our baser nature (i.e. lust, greed, power, etc.). Or they are presented by a "charismatic" personality that disarms us by his charm and personality.

We in leadership who are commissioned to care for the flock of God must have the ability to see through all this glitter and emotional hype. We must not be gullible. We have to examine just exactly what is being said, and what the end result of this teaching is going to be.

The men and women of Berea in Macedonia are prime examples of the right approach to "new truth." They were noble in that they searched the Scriptures daily to see whether the things Paul said were true (Acts 17:11). They were open-minded, but they were not gullible. There is a fine line here, but it can and should be maintained.

Genuine truth will always bear up under scrutiny.

Genuine truth will always bear up under scrutiny. The more you examine error, the weaker it becomes. But the more you examine truth the stronger it gets. If a leader refuses to be questioned, and says something like, "If you dare question me, you're attacking God's authority," or "We are God's voice to you, just obey," then you better watch out. Red danger flags should pop up.

There is another thing that needs to be done in this context. Not only should we study the doctrine itself, but we need to also see if those advocating this new doctrine are applying it "in truth." Remember, false teachers specialize in lying! Satan is a liar and the father of lies (John 8:44). The servants of Satan will speak "lies in hypocrisy" (I Timothy 4:2). There is a tendency for deceivers to preach just enough truth to make their whole system seem believable but when they apply it they often have very negative results.

Often deception is progressive. It begins with a subtle weakening of the authority of God's word. It soon begins to distort the word. From there it may even start to add to the scriptures. And finally, it lays aside the word of God. The end result of this process is always tragedy, despair and destruction.

Let me make one more application of this principle of studying a particular emphasis through to its end. Just as commercial advertising likes to associate its product with the sensational and the spectacular and attempts to seduce us into buying a second rate product simply by this association, so also people with a Pentecostal background are sometimes led astray by relying on the sensational ministry of signs, wonders and charismatic gifts.

Maintaining **BALANCE** *when winds of doctrine blow*

Human nature feeds on the demonstration of the supernatural. It likes the "out-of-the-ordinary" spectacular working of miracles. And sometimes, if we do not come with what some would see as a mighty manifestation of the Spirit, the people are disappointed. For this reason ministers can be tempted to start promoting the supernatural to a point that is way out of balance. They can actually pervert the gifts of the Spirit in order to please people. Jeremiah lamented this practice:

> *"The prophets prophesy falsely, and the priests bear rule by their [own] means; and My people love to have it so..."*
> *(Jeremiah 5:31).*

Leaders can fear that people will desert them if they fail to produce something spectacular. The people are conditioned to think that unless something unusual happened that they really did not have a good church service. Pastors can feel this pressure and attempt to manufacture "supernatural" happenings.

See what the end result is, not just what they say it will be.

I love the miraculous as much as anyone. I am a Charismatic through and through. I prophesy, pray for the sick and expect miracles and every other good thing that belongs in the House of God. But I do not make it the focus of the church or the ultimate test of faith. I do not live from one miracle to the next. In fact, I think it is good sometimes to have a service when nobody prophesies, just so these things do not become commonplace and ritualistic.

We come to the corporate gathering to enjoy the presence of Jesus. And He is there whether we see miracles happen or not. Jesus is there and that is what is important.

If we come for the miraculous and the miraculous becomes too commonplace it will not be long until the "experiences" of the past will no longer satisfy. Then people will begin to look for something that is yet more spectacular. When that gets dull for them, they will go on a search once again. In order for them to stay satisfied they must work up to heavier and heavier doses of the miraculous.

You may have the supernatural being manifest in your congregation, and if the people are focusing on the miraculous rather than their relationship to the Lord they will be satisfied for a season. But pretty soon someone else is going to come to town with a more spectacular ministry. Before long your ministry will be judged as "Ichabod" and the sheep will follow after this new ministry who lengthens legs or makes balls of fire appear. This ministry will satisfy their curiosity for a while. But soon they will be looking elsewhere. Sheep are vulnerable to a false or corrupt minister who promises even greater miracles. Sheep that have been conditioned in this way will very likely head off in his direction.

I have seen this happen. The false minister starts teaching things that are harmful to the church. He runs down the need for

Maintaining **BALANCE** *when winds of doctrine blow*

elders. He introduces new doctrines. And the people are so caught up in signs and wonders that they can not see the deception. When you try to warn them they respond, "But he's got to be of God, just look at all the miracles" (II Thessalonians 2:9, Revelation 13:13)!

Believers are not to follow after signs. Signs are to follow the believers (Mark 16:17)! Miracles and the charismatic gifts confirm the lordship of Christ. They show that Christ is on His throne dispensing gifts. They do not necessarily confirm the preacher! They do not prove that the minister is for real, only that the reign of Christ is for real (Ephesians 4:10-11, Acts 2:33, compare Acts 8:9-11, Matthew 7:21-23). The Bible warns us clearly of lying signs and wonders (II Thessalonians 2:9).

Eventually, even miracles by false ministers do not satisfy the craving of the miracle-minded people. They have had such large doses that they have now become desensitized. The fact that God has had compassion on a blind man and given him sight no longer produces any feelings. It no longer stimulates a greater appreciation for God. It does not result in a spirit of spontaneous worship to the Lord. The "goose bumps" are not there any more. At this point people may lose interest in going to church altogether. You can only hold an emotional high for so long and then you get overfed or saturated to the point that nothing stirs you any more.

Sheep are vulnerable to a false or corrupt minister who promises even greater miracles.

In maintaining balance in the church we want the Holy Spirit to move. We want to be open to the miraculous. But we must not become the initiators in this realm. Our duty is to give the Holy Spirit opportunities. He will sovereignly move. We do not have to work the people up to a high level of emotional pitch. But if you do start down that road, let me warn you, it is going to lead to a dead end. I think if you study this carefully and think this through to its logical conclusion, you will have to agree. Miracles are valid, but an over-emphasis on them in the final analysis will not produce what Christ intended for His church to enjoy.

This is a good way to analyze any particular doctrine. Study the teaching through to its logical conclusion and see if that is where you want to take your local body. See if the end product is the edification of the believers and the glorification of the Lord Jesus Christ (Ephesians 4:16, 3:21). That is the primary result that I am sure we all want!

LET OTHERS TRY IT FIRST

To maintain a well-balanced church, be patient. When there is something going through the country, wait, be patient and let other churches try it first! Sometimes pastors may be a little reluctant to do this because they do not want to appear to be "behind the times" in any way. Because of this it is easy for an

Maintaining **BALANCE** *when winds of doctrine blow*

insecure pastor to jump at everything that comes and as a result he becomes the "spiritual guinea pig" that will test this new emphasis. For the sake of your people and the long term stability of your church, however, it is better to adopt a "wait and see" attitude. That seems simple enough. But it may save you a lot of needless stress and many problems. Watch what is happening in the churches that are attempting to practice this truth and see how well they are doing. See if the implementation of that doctrine really works.

As pastors we are dealing with people's lives and souls. And I personally do not want to be responsible for treating the sheep as "guinea pigs." I want to stick to things that are tested and sure that I know are going to benefit them. I do not want to practice when people's lives are at stake. I want to emphasize doctrines that I know are proven to bring edification to the church.

I remember one man who came to Portland and wanted to hold meetings in our church. He came with a "new revelation." His revelation was that ultimately everyone was going to get saved, including the devil. He based it on a passage in a letter to Timothy:

"Who will have all men to be saved, and to come unto the knowledge of the truth" (I Timothy 2:4).

I personally do not want to be responsible for treating the sheep as "guinea pigs."

Needless to say, I had a few questions to ask him. I was particularly interested to find out exactly what was going on in his group. I discovered that there were loose morals, adultery and many serious problems. The fruit that the teaching of this doctrine produced was that sin had free reign among their people. I began to investigate further about his own personal life and found out what I had suspected all along. He was twisting the Word and had come up with a "new doctrine" in order to cover up for his own lasciviousness! He was not only deceived, but he was ruining other precious lives by this doctrine. Needless to say, he did not preach in our church, nor did we implement his "new revelation." By seeing what was going on in the other church we saved our own people from an extreme imbalance.

It might be well to note that a lot of so-called "new revelations," "new interpretations," or "new doctrines," are not "new" at all. Many of these "new" revelations have been around for centuries. They are in many cases only a revival of heresies of old. We can scan the pages of church history and see how a particular doctrine effected the churches. Hopefully by doing this we can learn from history.

Maintaining **BALANCE** *when winds of doctrine blow*

Doctrinal emphases do tend to come and go in cycles. We often find that the historical church also had to deal with those who advocated this "new" doctrine. By reading about their handling of the matter we can usually know what fruit this teaching is going to produce in our modern churches. If we learn from the past we often can save ourselves and our flock a lot of needless heartache.

TRY THE SPIRITS

The next principle that will help us stay flowing in the main channel of the river of God is given to us by the Apostle John:

"Beloved, believe not every spirit, but try the spirits whether they are of God; because many false prophets are gone out into the world" (I John 4:1).

We are told to try or test the spirits, because there are many deceivers. This is an important principle. Sometimes the false ministers are so "slick" and so persuasive in their presentations that it takes spiritual discernment to reveal their intentions.

In the letter to the Philippians Paul said to "beware of dogs, beware of evil workers, beware of concision" (Philippians 3:2). But in the first chapter he laid down the "means" of knowing and identifying who is "a dog":

Discernment is the key! Spiritual discernment.

"And this I pray, that your love may abound yet more and more in knowledge and in all judgment [Greek, aisthesei = discernment] so that ye may approve things that are excellent..." (Philippians 1:9).

Discernment is the key! Spiritual discernment. In the Septuagint translation of the Old Testament this Greek word discernment is found in Proverbs 1:22 and 2:10. It is the ability to judge by more than external facts alone.

"When wisdom entereth into thine heart, and knowledge is pleasant unto thy soul, discretion shall preserve thee, understanding shall keep thee;

To deliver thee from the way of the evil man, from the man that speaketh froward things;

Who leaves the paths of uprightness, to walk in the ways of darkness; who rejoice to do evil, and delight in the frowardness of the wicked; whose ways are crooked, and they froward in their paths" (Proverbs 2:10-15).

This discernment ability is what will save us from evil men. We in leadership need it to protect the flock. Discernment is that for which Solomon prayed (I Kings 3:9). And it was a characteristic that was to mark the ministry of the Messiah:

"And the spirit of the LORD shall rest upon Him, the spirit of wisdom and understanding, the spirit of counsel and might, the spirit of knowledge and of the fear of the LORD;

Maintaining
BALANCE
when winds
of
doctrine
blow

*And shall make him of quick under-
standing in the fear of the Lord; and He
shall not judge after the sight of His eyes,
neither reprove after the hearing of His
ear..." (Isaiah 11:2-3).*

It is almost mandatory, in considering a
person for eldership in a local church, that the
candidate have the ability to discern spirits.
Bible colleges need to impart into their
graduates discernment skills, in addition to
dispensing facts and figures about the books of
the Bible.

A major secular university's president
recently stated that business leaders and
professionals are concerned that universities,
while advancing technology, are not teaching
the virtues of "critical judgment."[2] They excel
in giving information, but are deficient in
wisdom. A wisdom that discerns "wrong
answers and cheap answers." A wisdom that
looks at all evidence, even the evidence that
does not fit your bias or ideology. A wisdom
that values ethics and intellectual integrity.[3]

*Sometimes you
can have the
right message
but it can be
delivered in
the wrong spirit.*

When a person approaches our church
with a new emphasis, our gift of discernment
should go into action. It is a gift given to the
church and we need to use it (I Corinthians
12:10). We need to ask ourselves, "In what
spirit is this man approaching us?" "What spirit
permeates his character?" "What spirit is
predominant in his message?" "What spirit will
rise up when this message is applied?"

Sometimes you can have the right message but it can be delivered in the wrong spirit. And that spirit will produce an effect in the congregation. That wrong spirit will be duplicated over and over.

When Jesus and His disciples were passing through Samaria on their way to Jerusalem, the villagers on one occasion did not receive them with hospitality. James and John asked the Lord if they should call fire down on them and destroy them! Jesus rebuked them sharply, "Ye know not what spirit ye are of!" (Luke 9:55). Now they had the right message. They preached the kingdom of God and that Jesus was Messiah. But their spirit was wrong. They were not presenting the message in the "atmosphere of the kingdom," which is "righteousness, peace and joy in the Holy Spirit" (Romans 14:17).

It does not matter how deep a revelation may seem, or how spectacular an emphasis may be, if it moves people away from righteousness, peace and joy, look out! I do not care how many scriptures they give for their "heavy" revelation. If it is so heavy that it takes away your joy, look out! If it produces fear instead of peace, look out!

This is precisely what Paul was teaching in Romans. The brothers in Rome were getting over bearing and over zealous in pushing some of their doctrines concerning the abolition of ceremonial laws through Christ,

Maintaining
BALANCE
when winds
of
doctrine
blow

and in observing certain holidays. Listen to what he wrote:

> *"But if thy brother be grieved with thy meat, now walkest thou not <u>charitably</u>. Destroy not him with thy meat, for whom Christ died.*
>
> *Let not then your good be evil spoken of, for the kingdom of God is not meat and drink; but <u>righteousness</u>, and <u>peace</u>, and <u>joy</u> in the Holy Ghost.*
>
> *For he that in these things serveth Christ is <u>acceptable</u> to God, and <u>approved</u> of men.*
>
> *Let us therefore follow after the things which make for peace, and things wherewith one may <u>edify</u> another"* (Romans 14:15-19).

Remember, we are talking about discernment. Paul discerned that these men were teaching some things which may, in and of themselves, not be wrong, but the intolerant and insensitive spirit in which they were presenting this teaching was "destroying" other brothers, and that is never acceptable. It produces imbalance.

The spirit that is acceptable and approved is a spirit that "makes for peace" and "edifies"

The spirit that is acceptable and approved is a spirit that "makes for peace" and "edifies" (verse 19). That is the spirit that keeps the church flowing in the main stream of the river of God.

I once was given some advice in pastoring by an elderly statesmen and experienced patriarch of the faith in Canada. He said, "If a young man, or a new minister, comes to your church and jumps up and starts prophesying, tell him to sit down. Then watch him. If he submissively sits down, and he is humble about it, you have a good man there. Let him minister."

"But if he gets upset, and starts to become riled up, defensive and mad, then keep your eye on him. He has a bad spirit, and may cause the church some problems!"

Now, I do not recommend you follow this practice, but it can be an effective way of testing the spirits. And we are commanded to test the spirits.

PROMOTE LOVE AND CHARITY

All of the other principles for maintaining balance in a church emanate from the principle of "showing the love of God." In the following scriptures notice how love is tied in with all the doctrines and practices of the church:

Maintaining **BALANCE** *when winds of doctrine blow*

"And though I have the gift of prophecy, and understand all mysteries and all knowledge; and though I have all faith so that I could remove mountains, and have not charity, I am nothing" (I Corinthians 12:2).

"Follow after charity, and desire spiritual gifts..." (I Corinthians 14:1).

"Watch ye (discernment), stand fast in the faith (doctrines), quit you like men, be strong. Let all your things be done with charity" (I Corinthians 16:13-14).

"We are bound to thank God always for you, brethren, as it is meet, because that your faith groweth exceedingly (doctrine), and the charity of every one of you all toward each other aboundeth" (II Thessalonians 1:3).

"But ye, building up yourselves on your most holy faith (doctrine), praying in the Holy Ghost, keep yourselves in the love of God..." (Jude 21).

"And if any man obey not your word by this epistle (doctrine), note that man, and have no company with him, that he may be ashamed. Yet count him not as an enemy, but admonish him as a brother. Now the Lord of peace himself give you peace always by all means" (II Thessalonians 3:14-16).

We need to maintain the climate of love in our churches

The New Testament writers did not hesitate to stand up for purity in doctrine. Perhaps we ministers in the twentieth century need to emulate their example more diligently. In essentials they were unswerving.

But in non-essentials they were sensitive, and tolerant. There were certain things that were not worth causing division over. They were not worth creating strife for. They were not worth offending a brother or making someone stumble.

But in all things the love of God was to be the primary motivation. And today, we need to maintain the climate of love in our churches. If we do not agree on a non-essential doctrine, we need to put it up on a shelf for a while until "cooler heads prevail." If a brother is wrong in doctrine or practice, we must approach him in humility and love, not arrogance (Galatians 6:1). If a false teacher is approaching the flock, out of love for the flock we must confront.

I am not talking about a loose type of love that allows things to enter into the church that should not be there. Love without truth is permissiveness, and we do not want that (Romans 6:1). But the Bible teaches about a love that stands up for the truth, a love that is willing to go to the cross for it, and all the while maintains a spirit of grace, forgiveness and trust in God. I think that is the kind of love we all want so that our churches will stay in balance and become what God intended His glorious body to be.

"Seeing ye have purified your souls in obeying the truth through the Spirit unto unfeigned love of the brethren, see that ye

Maintaining **BALANCE** *when winds of doctrine blow*

love one another with a pure heart fervently" (I Peter 1:22).

If this approach to settling differences had permeated the whole church world over the centuries, what a dynamic impact it would have had on unbelievers.[4] Church history could have been written with a lot more success stories! The salt would not lose its savor with such Christian charity. We need to follow this example and promote the spirit of love in our churches and fellowships while we are maintaining balance.

Love without truth is permissiveness

FOUR

DISCERNING IMBALANCE

The Bible often refers to doctrinal emphases as winds (Ephesians 4:14). Winds can be positive or they can be negative. On the positive side winds that come gently and in the right proportion can bring refreshing. They can be very desirable when they are in control. In fact, in Bible times, favorable winds were necessary for all movement or navigation on the high seas. So when the winds were under control and properly channeled they were a great benefit and seen as a great blessing.

In relation to the church, the Holy Spirit is seen as the wind or breath of God. In this regard the Holy Spirit moves as the wind purging, cleansing, guiding and impelling the church to the desired destination. The way in which the Spirit moves the church forward is by moving upon individuals and pouring out understanding and illumination concerning the purposes of God. As people respond to that impetus of the Spirit and begin moving in

Maintaining
BALANCE
when winds
of
doctrine
blow

response to the leading of the Spirit the church moves forward in a positive way.

However, the same winds that bring refreshing and guidance can also bring havoc and destruction if they come from the wrong direction or with intensified force. It is possible for man to take something that the Spirit is doing and pervert it with improper motivation or add to its intensity with human effort so that something that was indeed born of the Spirit can become driving and destructive. When doctrinal emphases get out of control or when they are controlled by man's energy they can become destructive.

As pastors we are constantly challenged to discern the winds. We must watch the winds and be prepared to discern between the good and the evil (Hebrews 5:14). We have to determine what is born of the Spirit and what is perpetuated by the efforts of man. We want to be open to the moving of the Spirit for growth and positive change, but we want to be cautious and resistant to that which is born of the flesh. The flesh profits nothing.

The same winds that bring refreshing and guidance can also bring havoc and destruction

As pastors, if we are to effectively discern the winds we need to read the signals that accompany the winds. We need to be able to identify the signs of the moving of the Spirit and the signs of turbulent winds.

WARNING SIGNS

Most of the time there are red flags or warning signs that can serve as signals in helping us discern the winds of doctrine that blow upon the church. Within most of these "winds" there is a pure element or something that God is trying to say, but by using certain means of testing we will be able to keep these winds from becoming hurricanes that could potentially destroy the ship.

Some of these signals are things that we have already discussed and will serve us by way of summarization. Others are given here so that we will have the necessary equipment to "test the spirit" or "test the winds."

1. **Watch out for the word "new" especially when associated with "revelation" (Ecclesiastes 1:9).**

God usually has a word or truth that He is emphasizing in the present for feeding, growth and development of His church. However, the present emphasis of the Spirit is never a new "revelation." God's revelation to man is complete in the Word of God, the Bible. The Spirit of God may bring new understanding or new illumination concerning the revealed Word of God, but everything we do in the present tense must be firmly rooted in the Bible. Any prophecy, revelation or insight which does not find its basis firmly in the Word of God must be rejected. "New" is

Maintaining
BALANCE
when winds
of
doctrine
blow

not always better. In fact, in the next chapter we will see that certain timeless truths must be the anchors that keep us from slipping into error.

2. **Watch out for anything that requires "private interpretation" (II Peter 1:20, II Corinthians 11:1-4).**

The Gospel is basically simple. God has designed His salvation in such a way that it can be received by all. We must be on guard when man would seek to complicate the Gospel or attempt to move us away from the simplicity of the Gospel.

Proud individuals will at times seek to make people overly dependent upon them for the "correct" interpretation of the Bible. They would make Christianity a secret order where it could only be successfully lived by having someone "in the know" disciple you. There are those who would seek to take the Bible out of the hands of common man and set themselves up as the authorized interpreters of the Bible.

Everything we do in the present tense must be firmly rooted in the Bible.

The spiritual things of the Lord are open to anyone who will come to God in humility and openness of Spirit. True ministers of the Gospel will lead people to Christ rather than make people dependent upon themselves.

3. **Watch out for those who major on the minors (II Corinthians 13:1).**

Whenever someone uses one or two obscure passages to develop a whole system of thought, a red flag should go up. God Himself indicates that every word needs to be established in the mouth of two or three witnesses. Often times a person will have developed a system of thought and then try to find a scripture or verse to support their position. This is not operating with a spirit of integrity before the Word of God.

True doctrinal pursuit should begin with the Bible before a system of thought is developed. We must say what the Bible says. We are not to try to make the Bible say what we say.

When we do discover truth we must be constantly attempting to balance that truth with other biblical truth. To do this we must give the most attention to that which the Bible gives the most attention. We must focus on what the Bible focuses on.

4. **Watch for extremes or truth out of balance (Matthew 7:14).**

Jesus spoke of the narrow way that leads to life. In relation to doctrine, the narrow way is often the mid-line between two extremes, the built in balance of biblical doctrine. Almost every concept has a balancing concept that helps keep everything in harmony.

Maintaining **BALANCE** *when winds of doctrine blow*

For example, the concept on faith must be balanced by the scriptures on works. God's love must not be preached at the expense of God's wrath. God's mercy must be balanced by the concept of holiness and justice. Man's responsibility, if not tempered by the sovereignty of God, will lead to legalism. The sovereignty of God without the balance of human responsibility might lead to license. Being a royal son must be coupled with the concept of being an obedient servant. Blessing and prosperity must be linked arm in arm with repentance and sacrifice. These concepts must come forth balanced. It is the narrow way that leads to life.

Any time only one of these concepts is emphasized the body will be out of balance. A body that is out of balance is extremely vulnerable and is susceptible to falling.

This does not mean that God will not lead pastors to emphasize a certain aspect of truth during a certain season in the life of the church. But it does mean that after that truth has been emphasized it will once again be integrated back into the body of truth in a balanced way.

There is no short cut to character development and spiritual growth.

5. Watch out for the promise of "instant maturity" (Philippians 1:6; 3:12-16).

Maturity by its very definition implies a constant and a steady growth. Sanctification is a process that was begun when we were born again in Christ Jesus and it will continue right up to the second coming of Christ.

Many people today are looking for an instant cure for all of their difficulties. If I can solve all of my problems by casting out the demon, or chanting a certain phrase, or experiencing a certain prayer or fasting certain foods, then that would be wonderful.

People can run for this remedy or that remedy and never find what they are looking for because there is no instant cure for their problem. They are going to have to repent, mortify the works of the flesh, put on the armor of God, stir themselves up and fight the good fight of faith. And they are going to have to do this each and every day of their lives. There is no short cut to character development and spiritual growth.

6. **Watch out not to judge a spiritual truth or a ministry on the basis of external signs that follow (II Thessalonians 2:9).**

We have a tendency to glorify the miraculous. If we see miracles as signs and wonders accompanying a person's ministry we can easily accept what is being said without testing it objectively. People today love spiritual experiences.

It is important that we understand that the presence of the miraculous is not God's badge of approval on an entire message or ministry.

Maintaining **BALANCE** *when winds of doctrine blow*

The gifts of the Spirit are not marks of maturity. The gifts of the Spirit are not earned or deserved.

The Bible warns us that in the last days there will be false christs (anointeds), false prophets, deceiving spirits and lying signs and wonders (Matthew 24:3-5, 11, 24-26; I Timothy 4:1-2; II Peter 2:1-3; II Thessalonians 2:1-12).

We want to believe that God will confirm His word with signs following but not all signs are from God and the presence of signs and wonders in a person's ministry does not indicate that everything that he says is true. The Bible is still the ultimate test of all truth.

7. Watch out for practices that elevate emotional experiences above the principles of God's Word (II Peter 1:16-21).

At times people can consider visions, dreams and personal prophetic words to be more important than the Word of God. These types of Christians preface their remarks with phrases like "The Lord showed me..."; "I had this dream..."; or "I know what the Bible says, but in my case God has clearly shown me otherwise."

We must trust the Scripture above our own subjective experiences

Peter had some of the greatest experiences that any human being could have. The Mount of Transfiguration was one example. But he was able to say "we also have a prophetic word which is even more sure than this." He was of course referring to the Scripture. As Christians we must trust the Scripture above our own subjective experiences or we will get off balance.

8. Watch out for spiritual teachings that justify carnal desires (James 4:1-4).

There are certain things that have always and will always appeal to the carnal man. Everyone can get excited about driving Cadillacs especially if doing so can be a mark of spiritual maturity. If I can clothe my greed or covetousness in a cloak of spirituality and thereby justify it, this becomes very appealing to the flesh.

People have justified all sorts of things from adultery to drunkenness in the guise of spirituality. Taking obscure verses, refusing to balance them with other verses and twisting them to fit some spurious interpretation they themselves sin and they lead others into the same sin.

The flesh rebels against the concepts of selflessness, sacrifice for others, and laying down one's life. Words like "repentance, tribulation, affliction and suffering" are not a part of many people's vocabulary. If there is a way to reason around the cross and clothe our self centeredness in a spiritual sounding phrase then we can keep our carnal nature and our form of religion. We can keep our conscience placated.

Maintaining **BALANCE** *when winds of doctrine blow*

The fact is, however, that the cross is part of the gospel. Any attempt to minimize the cost of discipleship needs to be rejected. True biblical Christianity must prevail.

9. **Watch out for teachings that promote health, wealth, success and happiness with no mention of cost, pain, persecution and even personal loss (I Timothy 1:8, 4:5; Hebrews 11:32-39).**

The Bible teaches that the way to live is to die. The way to exaltation is humility. It teaches that all who live godly in Christ will suffer persecution. It teaches that we must through much tribulation enter the kingdom of God. Jesus said the world will hate you. Paul said:

"But in all these things approving ourselves as ministers of God, in much patience, in afflictions, in necessities, in distresses, in stripes, in imprisonments, in tumults, in labours, in watchings, in fastings; by pureness, by knowledge, by longsuffering, by kindness, by the Holy Ghost, by love unfeigned, by the word of truth, by the power of God, by the armour of righteousness on the right hand and on the left, by honour and dishonour, by evil report and good report: as deceivers, and yet true; as unknown, and yet well known; as dying, and behold, we live; as chastened, and not killed; as sorrowful, yet alway rejoicing; as poor, yet making many rich;

Any attempt to minimize the cost of discipleship needs to be rejected.

as having nothing, and yet possessing all things" (II Corinthians 6:4-10).

I am not suggesting that Christians are not to enjoy life and see many victories. I am only suggesting that whatever we do, we do for His glory and not our own.

10.   Watch out for teachings that will not work in every culture as easily as they do in America (I Corinthians 7:17).

God's truth cuts across all time zones and all cultures. God's word is eternal. If we are properly interpreting the Word of God there is no place that the principles of God will not work. There is only one Gospel. There is not an American Gospel, an African Gospel and a Gospel for Communist Countries. There is one Gospel of the Kingdom that is to go forth in all the world.

If anything that I am teaching and preaching will not work equally as well in third world countries as it does in America I need to re-examine what I am teaching. God's word is universal. My words can be greatly effected by the culture in which I live. Somehow in order to stay balanced I must extract that which is national from that which is biblical. God only promises to bless that which is biblical.

11.   Watch out for doctrines that side step confession, repentance, restitution and forsaking sin and that release you from

Maintaining
BALANCE
when winds
of
doctrine
blow

personal responsibility for your deeds (Proverbs 28:13).

Confession, repentance, restitution and forsaking sin are still the foundation of the Christian life. There are many today who are offering love, acceptance and forgiveness without the basis for truth established. Mercy and truth must meet together (Psalm 85:10). When they do not, true recovery never takes place.

12. Watch out for doctrines that diminish the power of the cross and the work of repentance in the life of the believer (I Corinthians 2:2).

There is a great deal of blending of psychology and Christianity today. There is a place for scientific study relative to man and how he functions. But only the Bible has the answer to the needs of man. It will not be in man's reason that we will glory but only in the cross of Christ. The blood of Christ will never lose its power.

Truth does not need to be defended.

Paul was a man educated in all the wisdom of man for his day but he made a determination to know nothing but Christ and Him crucified.

13. Watch out for doctrines that are not willing to be questioned and tested (I Thessalonians 5:21; I John 4:1).

Truth does not need to be defended. It will always bear scrutiny. Anyone who cannot be questioned without becoming enraged should be suspect. The Berean believers are commended in the Bible for their rigorous search of the scripture upon hearing the teachings of Paul (Acts 17:11).

The Bible instructs us to prove all things and to test the spirit. The spirit of a person who brings forth a certain teaching will tell you as much about the doctrine as the words themselves. We are to reject error but we are to hold fast to the truth.

14. Watch out for doctrines that lead to spiritual pride or exclusivism (Matthew 24:26-27).

There are those who are much like the gnostics of the early church who promoted the idea that they had a certain secret body of knowledge that made them greater than others. If you understood and believed like they did then you became part of an inner circle. There are teachers today that would divide the body of Christ into select groupings or companies. All of this teaching is divisive and produces schisms in the body. Paul tells us clearly that there is but "one body" (Ephesians 4:4).

15. Watch out for teachings that elevate or promote an individual above Christ (John 3:30).

Maintaining **BALANCE** *when winds of doctrine blow*

John the Baptist was the greatest prophet who ever lived and yet no one had any greater spirit of humility. His sole mission was to point people to Jesus. When this was accomplished he felt he was a true success. When evaluating a message ask yourself, "Who does this elevate? Who does this promote?"

16. Watch out when the vessel does not confirm the message (Matthew 7:15-20).

Any time a message is coming forth it is good to be a fruit inspector. You cannot just judge a truth on the sound made or the enticing words. You must examine the fruit in the lives of those who are promoting that truth and the fruit that it has produced in the lives of others and the church as a whole.

BALANCING THE WARNING

In sharing all of these warning signs I suppose it would be possible for us to become so skeptical and overly cautious that we would question everything and everyone. The Bible does indicate that we are to "prove all things" but it also says that we are to "hold fast to that which is good."

God uses winds to bring positive growth, change and movement.

In all of these guidelines we must remember that God uses winds to bring positive growth, change and movement. Most of the winds have a positive element of truth and contain something that God is really wanting us to hear. Those positive truths we must search out, believe, embrace and integrate into what we are doing. In this way we move forward from faith to faith.

Maintaining
BALANCE
when winds
of
doctrine
blow

FIVE

A BALANCED DIET

Just as sure as the sun rises in the east, I know that sooner or later in the near future another wave of some "new" theology will hit the shores of Christianity. In my years as pastor I have already seen wave after wave come and beat on the doors of our local churches. Many of our churches have survived and endured these storms of imbalance; but, sadly, many others have been swept away in these under-currents and have been lost in a whirlpool of destruction.

There has been "Hope Theology," "Kingdom Now Theology," "Liberation Theology," "Dominion Mandate Theology," "New Wave Theology," "Discipleship Theology," "Dispensational Theology," "Covenant Theology," "Faith and Prosperity Theology," "Inner Healing Theology," "Reformation Theology," and the list goes on and on.

Some of these have brought strength and direction to the church, and some have wrought

Maintaining **BALANCE** *when winds of doctrine blow*

havoc. Some have caused us to rethink and renew our commitment to a basic Christian doctrine, while others have been simply a revival of ancient error which has hurt the church world in the past.[5]

As a pastor I am deeply interested in any thing that will edify my congregation. I am not interested in anything that will cause the members to become unstable and roam aimlessly. I do not want anything that appeals only to my curiosity, or just tantalizes my desire for the sensational and emotional.

I want something that will produce steadfastness and stability that I can pass on to the sheep. I am sure we all want only those things that will prevent our people from being spiritual gadabouts, chasing after novel doctrines, and coveting sensational revelations. This was the character flaw of the Athenians of Paul's day:

> "For all the Athenians and strangers which were there spent their time in nothing else but either to tell, or to hear some new thing" (Acts 17:21).

Some of our church members have not had a balanced spiritual diet!

No one wants this Athenian spirit to scatter their own sheep. It will just waste their time and energy and possessions. All they will have to show for it are empty speculations, unfulfilled date-setting schemes, and disillusionment.

A HEALTHY DIET

Modern dietary research has discovered an interesting phenomenon. When a person stops eating three nutritional meals a day, at first they will feel sluggish. But then after a continual period of neglect, something else begins to happen. That person will soon become restless and fidgety, unsettled and flurried. He will always be on the go in a bustle of nervous activity. It is like he is driven by a nervous energy. He literally wears himself to a frazzle.

Such is the case with many children in our day. Much of their restlessness and continual roving and roaming about is due to their lack of proper nourishment. Many of them have no stability or self-control because their body (especially the nervous system) lacks the nutrients to maintain its equilibrium. There are many possible causes for any social behavior such as lack of discipline, lack of parental role models or prejudice. But this area of malnutrition must not be overlooked.

Likewise, when we come to the church, I think a lot of restlessness and spiritual roving is caused by this same thing. Some of our church members have not had a balanced spiritual diet! They are not stable or steadfast because they have not been fed properly. They have not been given all the "basic food groups" on which they need to grow.

Maintaining **BALANCE** *when winds of doctrine blow*

When a person has finished eating a well-balanced meal, he is satisfied. He has no craving to go after "junk food." The well nourished body is restful and strong. It will respond to the pressures of work during the day and be very productive.

So also is a church body. If the church body is fed with the essential, basic spiritual food groups, the people will not go chasing after all the junk food that "fly-by-night" vendors are marketing! They will not be spending nervous energy seeking "cotton-candy" doctrines. Instead, each well-fed joint will be supplying strength to the whole body, and it will be productive in the kingdom (Ephesians 4:16). Instead of being driven and weakened by the Athenian spirit which looks for novelties, the body will have a strong constitution and strength to carry on the work of the kingdom.

THE BASIC DOCTRINES

The Bible gives us the basic truths that we need to feed upon. It provides for us a balanced pattern for living the Christian life. And consequently, the congregations which are given this balanced diet of Christianity are less susceptible to being controlled by their feelings or led astray by their curiosities. They are more settled and grounded. And this settling is necessary to make it to the end:

The Bible gives us the basic truths that we need to feed upon.

"...to present you holy and unblameable and unreproveable in His sight, if ye continue in the faith grounded and settled, and be not moved away from the hope of the gospel which ye have heard..." (Colossians 1:22-23).

What are these essential and basic doctrines that are to be in a well-balanced church? I think the answer to that is found in the second chapter of the book of Acts. The people had just asked "What shall we do?" Peter gave an altar call and laid the foundation for the first local church. This was the beginning of the church.

But notice that Peter did not end his preaching and instruction after he spoke of repentance, baptism and the in-filling of the Holy Spirit. He continued speaking.

"And with many other words did he testify [charge] and exhort" (Acts 2:40).

Peter not only gave instructions for salvation, but he went on to instruct us about the basic things that should be in every local church. At this inauguration he was laying the groundwork and giving the pattern for us to follow. But what were these "many other words?"

That used to really bother me. "Why didn't Luke record the rest of those words? Since they are so important, and since they will

Maintaining **BALANCE** *when winds of doctrine blow*

keep the church balanced, why didn't Luke write them down for us? Surely he could have explained to us what they were!"

Then one day it dawned on me. I discovered how we can understand what those "many other words" were. In my mind, God took me to a football game. Eleven men go out onto a field to play, but before they make a move, they all gather together in a "huddle." They whisper something and plan the next play. Up in the bleachers, the crowd is wondering what they are saying. "I wonder what play the coaches called into the huddle? I wonder what the quarterback said?"

How can we know what was said? Simply by watching the next play! Just see what happens next on the field. So also, we can tell what Peter said by looking at what the "hearers" did next. Luke recorded these actions for us in verses forty-one through forty-seven. These coupled with the salvation message, are the basic truths or the foundational principles in which a well-balanced, well-rounded church should be grounded and settled. The pastor who leads his congregation into these basic areas will have a congregation that is feeding on a balanced spiritual diet! The congregation that heartily feeds upon these will have little time or desire to run after faddish trends in doctrine. They will be less vulnerable to winds of doctrine that would attempt to blow them off course.

Biblical repentance requires a change of mind.

REPENTANCE

First Peter called the people to repentance. Biblical repentance requires a change of mind. This meant that there needed to be a total change in the way they were thinking. Instead of going by their ideas and interpretations, they were now to think God's thoughts on each and every subject. It involved grief or sorrow for past conduct which resulted from that faulty human thinking (II Corinthians 7:9), and it involved an actual <u>turning from</u> that conduct (Acts 8:22) and a <u>turning to</u> a new way of thinking (Mark 1:15).[6]

It is this acknowledgement of sin and wrong-doing that is so vital to a healthy life. In this technological society people are told to do everything else (i.e. explain the situation away, blame someone else, accentuate the positive, attribute failures to heredity and environment, etc.), but they are not being told to repent! Repressed guilt feelings are a major contributor to mental disorders. Guilt needs to be dealt with, forgiven and cleansed. Then people can get on with living the victorious life God intended for them to have. What a clean feeling it is to lay your head down on your pillow at the end of a day and know that you are forgiven!

"Whosoever committeth sin is the servant of sin...If the Son therefore shall make you free, ye shall be free indeed" (John 8:34-36).

Maintaining
BALANCE
*when winds
of
doctrine
blow*

"Blessed is he whose transgression is forgiven, whose sin is covered. Blessed is the man unto whom the LORD imputeth not iniquity, and in whose spirit there is no guile" (Psalm 32:1-2, Romans 4:3-8).

A person who has a right understanding of repentance will be a very content individual. He will not be wandering like those who continually seek for something to satisfy and to cure the empty gnawing feeling of a guilt-ridden heart. He will be settled and grounded in God's deeply satisfying grace!

WATER BAPTISM

As an outward evidence and public confirmation of the inward work of God in their hearts and minds, the people were commanded to be baptized. By being baptized each one identified with the work of Christ on the cross and His subsequent resurrection (Romans 6:4). His old life of sin was considered dead, and a new life in Christ was now his to live!

This act of immersion also signified the fact that all people were being united as one in one body[7] (I Corinthians 12:13). Whether we be Gentile or Jew, rich or poor, slave or free, we are all members of the same body. The church is the original "melting pot" of all nationalities into one man which conforms to the image of Christ (Galatians 3:27-29).

When a person is a baptized believer he belongs to the greatest organization this world will ever know!

This gives each one of us identity. Church members do not have to run here or there searching for identity. Their identity is found in the body of Christ. This gives each baptized person in the world the highest possible sense of dignity! A Christian does not have to go running after this religious leader or that guru. He does not have to seek his identity in the wearing of a novel type of religious garment, or joining up with a faddish cult group (I Corinthians 1:8-16). No! When a person is a baptized believer he belongs to the greatest organization this world will ever know! He becomes part of a very special class of people, part of a royal priesthood, part of a unique race (I Peter 2:9)! He is a member, in a very special way, of the body of Christ!

HOLY SPIRIT BAPTISM

In ancient days God anointed only certain individuals with the miraculous power of the Holy Spirit. This anointing enabled them to carry out their function in a special way, whether they be prophet, priest, or king (I Kings 19:15-16). It was such a blessing that Moses yearned for the day when all the people would be anointed with the Holy Spirit (Numbers 11:29). One thousand years after Moses, the prophet Joel declared that that very thing would happen!

"And it shall come to pass afterward, that I will pour out my Spirit upon all

Maintaining
BALANCE
when winds
of
doctrine
blow

flesh; and your sons and your daughters will prophesy, your old men shall dream dreams, your young men shall see visions; and also upon the servants and upon the handmaids in those days will I pour out my Spirit" (Joel 2:28-29)!

According to the interpretation of Peter the apostle, this began to be fulfilled on the Feast of Pentecost. Jesus had said that when He ascended He would sit at the right hand of God, and ask God to give the gift of the Holy Spirit to His followers (Acts 1:4). And when the Spirit was poured out on the Day of Pentecost it was a sign or proof that Jesus was the ascended Lord (Acts 2:33)!

Today Jesus is still at the right hand of God reigning! And He is still pouring out the Holy Spirit upon believers. He is still dispensing all the spiritual gifts. He is still equipping His church for the work of the ministry. There is still a need in the church for these gifts, and I appreciate them.

MORE ESSENTIAL DOCTRINES

The baptism of he Holy Spirit is only a means to an end.

Since I was raised in classical Pentecostal church, I always read the second chapter of Acts with emphasis mainly on the first part where people were getting saved, baptized and filled with the Holy Spirit (Acts 2:38). We all thought that if we could get people saved and filled with the Spirit, that all of our problems would be solved.

However, if our teaching ends at this point we will have churches that are out of balance. The baptism of the Holy Spirit is only a means to an end. It is not an end in itself. All of the second chapter of Acts is important because it not only tells us about the salvation of each believer, but it also instructs us as to how these believers are going to relate to each other, as well as minister to the world. It shows how Christians can come together and form a well-balanced church body that will be a glory throughout the earth.

TEACHING

After Paul charged and exhorted with further words, the people "continued steadfastly in the apostles' doctrine" (Greek didache = teaching). What was the apostles' teaching? What was it all about? The rest of the book of Acts tells us:

"And daily in the temple, and in every house, they ceased not to teach and preach Jesus Christ" (5:42).

"And straightway he preached Christ in the synagogues, that he is the Son of God" (9:20).

"Paul also and Barnabas continued in Antioch, teaching and preaching the word of the Lord" (15:35).

Maintaining **BALANCE** *when winds of doctrine blow*

*"Did we not straitly command you that
ye should not teach in this name? And
behold, ye have filled Jerusalem with your
doctrine (didache)" (5:28).*

The apostles' doctrine was the teaching
about the centrality of Jesus Christ. Any
balanced spiritual diet must contain this
teaching. Pastors must continually point to
Jesus. They must continually lift Jesus up.
Lost souls must be directed to come to Jesus
and believers must be admonished to abide in
Jesus (John 15). Jesus is not a hope, but He
is the only hope for this world. So He must
remain the central point in all our teaching.
A strong church must be a teaching church.

Luke wrote that "they continued
steadfastly" in this teaching. The verb here is
in the imperfect tense signifying continuous
action. "They kept on continuing steadfastly."
Their whole life was involved and wrapped up
in the teaching and presentation of Christ. Any
congregation that does this is going to remain
"steadfast." Keeping Christ as the main focal
point of our teaching will prevent us from
wandering off out of the stream of God.

*Pastors must
continually
point to
Jesus.*

FELLOWSHIP WITH GOD

In a balanced church not only are the
people supposed to know about Christ, but they
are to have an on-going fellowship and
communion with Christ. Being saved is not

merely to involve a mental assent to a doctrinal creed, it involves having a personal relationship and fellowship with Jesus:

"God is faithful, by whom ye were called unto the fellowship of His Son, Jesus Christ our Lord" (I Corinthians 1:9).

"The grace of the Lord Jesus Christ, and the love of God, and the communion [fellowship] of the Holy Ghost, be with you all" (II Corinthians 13:14).

Church members are really missing out in the Christian life if they are just going through the motions of religious ceremony. The church is the house where God dwells. Humanly speaking, if I entered a person's house and ignored the man of the house, something would be drastically wrong.

What a privilege it is to have intimate communion and fellowship with God. And what a stabilizing factor it is in a life. There is no need to chase after some dazzling, fast-talking minister who happens to pop into town, when you can come into the presence of God and enjoy His fellowship and communion in His House!

"That which we have seen and heard declare we unto you, that ye also may have fellowship with us; and truly our fellowship is with the Father, and with His Son, Jesus Christ" (I John 1:3).

Maintaining **BALANCE** *when winds of doctrine blow*

BREAKING OF BREAD

The new disciples also continually observed the "breaking of bread." This important observance was symbolic of sin, discipline, and restoration. It was instituted by Christ the night He was betrayed (Matthew 26:26-29; Mark 11:22-25; Luke 22:14-20). It stands for the terrible penalty of sin, and the sacrifice of Christ to pay that penalty for us. The suffering, death, and shedding of blood of Jesus was the judgment of God on all our sins, and without it there was no remission of sins (Romans 6:23).

However, the beautiful thing is that this judgment was not to destroy, to condemn, or to annihilate, but it was to restore! The cross stood for death to the old life, but it made the way to a brand new life. Restoration of mankind and resurrection to life was the goal and the desired end result (I Peter 2:24).

When the "table of the Lord" ceases to be a part of the balanced spiritual diet of the church, corruption sets in.

That is why Paul emphasized the need for personal discipline and the need to pause and consider one's own standing before God when coming to the "table of the Lord" (I Corinthians 11:23-32). If a man examines himself, if he judges himself and repents of all sins, he will escape the judgment to come (I Corinthians 11:32). This reflective examination and discipline makes a church strong. It makes a church invincible.

But when a church starts to ignore the breaking of bread, and discipline breaks down, then the people are more prone to be carried away by their lusts (James 1:14). When the "table of the Lord" ceases to be part of the balanced spiritual diet of the church, corruption sets in. And when that happens the church loses its influence in the world.

God wants a church that is "a glorious church, not having spot, or wrinkle or any such thing; but that it should be holy and without blemish" (Ephesians 5:27). The Lord's Supper was not instituted to condemn but to convict, so that restoration might come, so that holiness might be restored. And where there is holiness there is power and influence!

PRAYERS

One thing that the Lord Jesus made unmistakably clear while on earth was that His house was to be a "house of prayer."

"Even them will I bring to my holy mountain, and make them joyful in my house of prayer; their burnt offerings and their sacrifices shall be accepted upon mine altar; for mine house shall be called an house of prayer for all people" (Isaiah 56:7).

"And [Jesus] said unto them, It is written, My house shall be called the house

Maintaining
BALANCE
when winds
of
doctrine
blow

of prayer; but ye have made it a den of thieves" (Matthew 21:13).

Jesus was a person of prayer, and the disciples recognized that John the Baptizer was also a man of prayer:

"And it came to pass, that as He was praying in a certain place, when He ceased, one of His disciples said unto Him, Lord, teach us to pray, as John also taught his disciples. And He said unto them, When ye pray, say Our Father..." (Luke 11:1-2).

The early church gave themselves to prayer. Every time there was a crisis, a decision to be made, elders to appoint, disputes to settle, direction to be taken, or any major event to transpire, the church resorted to prayer.

The letters of the apostles to the young local churches scattered throughout the Roman Empire are all full of admonitions to be "instant" in prayer, or to be "without ceasing" in prayer, or to "continue" in prayer (Romans 12:12, James 5:13, Colossians 4:2, I Thessalonians 5:17).

That which brings revival maintains revival.

Prayer is a priority in our local church. The prayer time before the meetings is not an option. Our church cannot survive without it. Praying revived the life of our church. And that which brings revival maintains revival.

"And the inhabitants of one city shall go to another, saying, Let us go speedily to pray before the Lord, and to seek the Lord of hosts; I will go also. Yea, many people and strong nations shall come to seek the Lord of hosts in Jerusalem, and to pray before the Lord" (Zechariah 8:21-22; compare Acts 2:5).

"Be careful [anxious] for nothing; but in everything by prayer and supplication with thanksgiving let your requests be made known unto God" (Philippians 4:6).

We have already mentioned the need for prayer in order to maintain balance in a previous chapter. But let me just state again that any time some new wind of doctrine blows your way, wait on God about it. Seek God about it. Find His direction and will. Taking time out to seek God just may save hours later of trying to repair damage or trying to save shipwrecked lives caused by an over-emphasis in doctrine. Watch and pray that ye enter not into temptation (Matthew 26:41).

FEAR OF GOD

In verse forty-three of the second chapter of Acts we find another thing that resulted from Peter's "many other words." It resulted in a fear that kept coming on each soul (person). "Came" is in the imperfect tense and denotes continuance and permanence. The

Maintaining
BALANCE
*when winds
of
doctrine
blow*

disciples walked in the fear of God daily. Luke makes reference to this many times throughout the Book of Acts (9:31, 13:26, 5:11, 19:17). Fear can be a healthy thing depending upon the subject of your fear. Fear can keep us from going too close to the edge of a cliff. It keeps us from sticking our hands in hot fire. It keeps us from becoming too daring.

But first and foremost we are to fear God. This is a major theme both in the Old Testament and in the New.

"Arise, shine; for thy light is come...Then thou shalt see, and flow together, and thine heart shall fear, and be enlarged" (Isaiah 11:1-3).

"A son honoreth his father, and a servant his master...and I be a master, where is my fear" (Malachi 1:6)?

"O fear the Lord, ye his saints: for there is no want to them that fear him" (Psalms 34:9-11).

"In the fear of the Lord is strong confidence...The fear of the Lord is a fountain of life, to depart from the snares of death" (Proverbs 14:26-27). (See also Luke 12:4-5).

Whatever one fears becomes a dominant force in his life.

Whatever one fears becomes a dominant force in his life. The heart that fears the Lord is committed to the Lord. There then is no room for compromise or neutrality with sin and evil conduct when you are aware of the presence of God and are in fear of Him (Proverbs 8:13). This healthy fear keeps us from being self-assertive, proud, and boastful. It continually reminds us that we will give account to God for all our actions and words. As a result of this it helps us treat our fellow man decently (Ephesians 5:21), restrains us from giving in to our baser nature, and keeps us from going off into extremes.

I mentioned that fear can be healthy depending on the object of that fear. We need to be sure that it is God that we are fearing, and not some one else that we should not be fearing. For instance, the Bible says we are not to fear false prophets (Deuteronomy 18:22), nor the face of man (Proverbs 29:25), nor man-made religions (Isaiah 29:13).

A lot of men who lead people astray use fear as one of their tools. They appeal to man's fears to push their false doctrines, or they use fear of violence to dominate their lives. Talking to those who have been involved in cults or in an extreme group, they invariably mention the spirit of fear that prevailed over them.

But a people who fear God, and God alone, will not be easy prey for these false prophets. A church that trains its members to stand up for truth without fear or favor of men will remain balanced. We need to make sure

Maintaining
BALANCE
when winds
of
doctrine
blow

that a healthy fear of God is one of the essential teachings maintained in our local churches.

SIGNS AND WONDERS

Another basic area of church life listed in this second chapter of Acts was the continual working of signs and wonders. Signs and wonders were given to the church as part of the "grace gifts" from the Lord (I Corinthians 12:28). They were inseparable from the preaching and teaching of the ministers portrayed in the Book of Acts (Acts 4:30, 5:12, 6:8, 14:3). Besides general statements concerning the working of miracles, Luke gave several specific examples of them. People were raised from the dead (9:41), struck dead (5:5), freed from prison bars (5:19), freed from demons (8:7), healed from lameness (3:7), given sight (9:12), blinded (13:11), and miraculously preserved (28:3-6).

Signs and wonders have not ceased from the church.

But in these cases, the miracles were sought with right motives and were the result of the "hearing of faith" (Galatians 3:5). They were not a means of getting money (8:18), nor a demonstration of human power (14:11-15), nor a result of hypocritical ritual (19:13-16). Miracles are to be done by tapping into the mind of the Lord and walking in it and not acting in presumptuous faith (John 8:28-29, 5:19).

Signs and wonders have not ceased from the church. There will always be a need for them. People continually get sick. The word still needs confirming (Mark 1:17-20). Society still needs to know that the Kingdom of God has come (Luke 11:20). And there is an on-going need for church members to see the demonstration of God's power.

Signs and wonders are to be included as one of the basic, essential parts of church life. Too often churches have ignored this, and it has opened the door for the sheep to be tempted to run off in search for them. They leave the protection of the local ministry and run off with the first revivalist who can perform the miraculous. Not all the blame can be laid on the innate desire of people to want the sensational and spectacular. Often it is because we have failed to exercise faith and believe God for the miraculous in our own local churches. This can leave a void, into which all sorts of extremism quickly comes. The miraculous needs to be the work of all the local ministries <u>with proper teaching and direction accompanying it</u>. When done in this manner it brings edification to the church and keeps everything in proper balance.

COMMON WELFARE

The next basic essential that pervaded the church in Acts and continued on and on was the spirit of caring and common welfare. "All

Maintaining
BALANCE
*when winds
of
doctrine
blow*

that believed were together and had all things common" (2:44, "had" is in the continuous imperfect tense).

To make sure no one was in need of food or shelter, those that had extra land and real estate and extra personal property, sold them and turned the money in to the church ministers for distribution (2:45). The text does not imply that they sold the homes that they needed to live in. This was not communal living, nor was it communism--it was a caring community.

Paul explained this principle in the second book of Corinthians as "equality" (II Corinthians 8:14). Those whom God had blessed with abundance willingly gave to those in want. There was no covetousness or greed in the early church (Acts 5:1-11). Instead a spirit of liberality prevailed.

Examples of giving "to the necessities of the saints" are abundant throughout the New Testament church. Some churches, like the one at Philippi, often gave beyond what they could really afford to give (II Corinthians 8:1-3). But it was a constant concern of all the churches and their leaders that the poor, the widow, and disaster victims be cared for:

This was not communal living, nor was it communism – it was a caring community.

> *"Agabus...signified by the spirit that there would be great dearth throughout all the world...Then the disciples, every man*

according to his ability, determined to send relief" (Acts 11:28-29).

"Look not every man on his own things, but every man also on the things of others" (Philippians 2:4; Romans 12:13).

"Pure religion and undefiled before God and the Father is this, to visit the fatherless and widows in their affliction" (James 1:27).

"But to do good and to communicate [goods] forget not; for with such sacrifices God is well pleased" (Hebrews 13:16; Galatians 2:10).

Jesus carried the concept of giving still further. He taught that we are to give even to those who could never reciprocate by later giving back to our needs:

"Then said he also to him...When thou makest a dinner or a supper, call not thy friends, nor thy brethren, neither kinsmen, nor thy rich neighbors; lest they also bid thee again, and a recompense be made thee. But when thou makest a feast, call the poor, the maimed, the lame, the blind: And thou shalt be blessed..." (Luke 14:12-14).

To see how close to the heart of God the poor and suffering are, we need only recall that

Maintaining
BALANCE
when winds of doctrine blow

Sodom was destroyed not primarily for immorality, though that was bad, but because she neglected the poor and needy (Ezekiel 16:49)! The Israelites were ejected from the Promised Land because they did not support the elderly and poor in violation of the fifth commandment (Exodus 20:12, Ephesians 6:2). It is ironic that those Israelites that neglected the poor out of covetousness were all taken captive into exile, and only "the poorest sort of the people of the land" were allowed to remain in the Promised Land (II Kings 24:14).

He that has pity on the poor is really lending to the Lord (Proverbs 19:17), and those that do not have such pity endanger their own well-being (Proverbs 17:5, 22:16).

There is one more aspect of common welfare that sets Christianity apart from all other religions. We are not only to share with our brothers and sisters, we are not only to share with our unsaved neighbors, but we are also to have compassion on our enemies! "If thine enemy be hungry, give him bread to eat; and if he be thirsty, give him water to drink" (Proverbs 25:21, Matthew 5:44, Romans 12:20). In all three of these aspects, such giving brings glory to God and His house (II Corinthians 9:13). Common welfare and charity are to be basic elements in our local churches.

It is this common welfare principle that many cults and extreme groups have capitalized on to draw in unsuspecting people. A lot of

Common welfare and charity are to be basic elements in our local churches.

their public relations brochures give the picture of their group as being one big happy family where no one is in need. Or where they have a huge welfare department that supposedly meets every member's needs. Some of these images are simply false advertising. Some pretty pictures painted by these groups are tainted by accompanying extremes such as authoritarian control and a lack of personal freedom.[8]

But regardless of their abuses, our local churches are to take care of our own hurting members. This is to be an essential part of our churches. People should not have to seek charity and security elsewhere. We should not be giving the cults this opening by being deficient in our duty to our people. A church is out of balance if it says "God bless you," but doesn't meet the needs of the hurting (James 2:15-16; Matthew 25:31-46). But by fulfilling our duty we will be accomplishing two good deeds! Not only will we be meeting needs, but we will be preventing people from running off to extremes.

UNITY WITH DIVERSITY

Verse forty-six of this second chapter of Acts reports that the believers were "with one accord" in the temple courts daily. We had already been told that on the Day of Pentecost they were all "with one accord" (Acts 2:1). This deep spiritual fellowship of believers with

Maintaining
BALANCE
when winds
of
doctrine
blow

one another is basic to the effectiveness of a church.

Jesus taught that a "house divided against itself" cannot last very long (Matthew 12:25). A house that is going to last must have unity of fellowship. When the early church came together, Luke wrote that they did it "with one accord," whether it was to pray, to discuss problems, or to respond to preaching (Acts 2:1, 2:26, 4:24, 4:32, 1:14, 5:12, 8:6, 15:25). This was not a mechanical unity, but a unity of the Spirit, rising out of the heart of the people:

> *"Fulfill ye my joy, that ye be likeminded, having the same love, being of one accord, of one mind" (Philippians 2:2).*

> *"...that ye stand fast in one spirit, with one mind striving together for the faith of the gospel" (Philippians 1:27).*

> *"Finally brethren...be of one mind, be in peace" (II Corinthians 13:11).*

> *"Finally, be ye all of one mind, having compassion one of another" (I Peter 3:8).*

> *"That ye may with one mind and one mouth glorify God" (Romans 15:6, 12:16).*

> *"Now I beseech you...that ye all speak the same thing, and that there be no division among you; but that ye be perfectly*

A house that is going to last must have unity of fellowship.

joined together in the same mind and in the same judgment" (I Corinthians 1:10).

There are times in church life when there are disagreements concerning doctrines and practices--the apostolic church certainly had their share. But we are to endeavor "to keep the unity of the Spirit in the bond of peace...till we all come in the unity of the faith" (Ephesians 4:3,13).

How do you know if you are in unity or not? When you are dwelling in unity you are sensitive to your brother's and sister's emotions. When my toes are stepped on, my whole body screams out in pain. When my eyes are delighted, my heart excites the whole body. By one Spirit we have been baptized into one body (I Corinthians 12:13). We are all differing members of one body. And when something happens to another member of our body, if we are in unity, we too will be involved. If individuals in a local church cannot feel the hurts of the wounded or rejoice in the successes of others, they are lacking in this unity.

Unity is a basic ingredient that God has put into His church to cause it to be glorious. The church is to be a place where we love one another, share life together, minister to one another. The early Christians went to prison together, they suffered together, they walked together, they believed together, they sang together, and they prayed together.

Maintaining **BALANCE** *when winds of doctrine blow*

Any time a tragedy strikes the church, or a disagreement arises concerning some policy, or a church faces a strategic time of decision, all the members of the church should rally to the occasion, and all should adopt the common cause of quickly restoring the unity of fellowship! God is glorified in that!

This principle found in the twelfth chapter of First Corinthians transformed my whole outlook on church life, my attitude to fellow ministers, and my relationship to other church members. No matter how different we are to each other, we need each other! I realized that I actually needed people who were definitely different from me to help me effectively minister to the church. Our church needed the ministry of the pastor. True. But the sheep also need the ministry of the prophet, and the evangelist, and some good teachers, and administrators, and helpers and the other ministries of the body. And though each ministry is different, yet that differing gives strength to our church. Just like the diverse members of our physical body all pulling together make for a very practical organism that can perform a wide range of tasks![9]

This concept of the early church as a team ministry or body ministry all functioning in the unity of fellowship, and with a common cause, is vital to having a balanced church (I Corinthians 12:27-30).

No matter how different we are to each other, we need each other!

I believe a lot of church fights could have been avoided, a lot of schisms could have been mended, and a lot of splinter groups would not have gone off on their own little tangents, if they all would have seen the importance of maintaining "unity with diversity." I believe there would be a lot less imbalance in some churches if differing ministries were allowed to exist side by side in unity.

Some churches are out of balance because they have grabbed on to a particular style or type of ministry that is popular at that given moment. What usually happens a few years later is that another type of ministry becomes popular and the sheep flock to this new wave of ministry and try it for a few years. This cycle can happen over and over again. God's desire is that ministries function together in the local church at the same time. This is the only way that the diversity of needs among the sheep can be met. God's plan involves the unity of fellowship with the diversity of ministry and membership. That approach brings balance and health to the House of God.[10]

JOYOUS CONTENTMENT

Another element of the balanced diet of church life is "enthusiastic joy." The disciples had enthusiasm for life, abounding joy, and rejoicing hearts. The author of Acts wrote that in each home the believers ate with gladness and sincerity (2:46).

Maintaining
BALANCE
when winds
of
doctrine
blow

"Gladness" hardly does the Greek word justice. The word used here means "extreme joy." It was used by Luke when the angel told Zacharias that he would have "joy and gladness; and many shall rejoice at this [John's] birth" (Luke 1:14). And again he used it when "the babe [John] leaped in Elizabeth's womb for joy" at the arrival of Mary, pregnant with the Messiah (Luke 1:44)! A form of this word is also used in Mary's Magnificat: "My soul doth magnify the Lord, and my spirit hath rejoiced in God my Savior" (Luke 1:46-46). It was also said that Christ was anointed with the "oil of gladness" (extreme joy) above His fellows (Hebrews 1:9; see also Jude 24).

This unquenchable joy accompanied the disciples in each of their homes continually while they ate together.[11] This exuberant joy was the mark of the presence of God in their midst. It enveloped their daily living.

You cannot manufacture on-going joy like this. This is an inner contentment, independent of circumstances, which is based on a vital relationship with the Lord. The Christian that is alive with the Spirit of Christ can carry on life's tasks, face any circumstance and adversity, and still have a deep-seated joy and peaceful rest.

If you do not have joy, it will cost you.

Once you have a thriving church going, the first thing Satan will try to do is destroy the joy. He will attempt to kill the enthusiasm and the excitement of being in the presence of

God. When joy withers, there is fruitlessness (Joel 1:9-12) and loss of strength (Nehemiah 8:10). Notice that the reason the Israelites perished was that they did not serve the Lord with gladness and a joyful heart (Deuteronomy 28:47).

If you do not have joy, it will cost you. It will cost you your family. It will cost you your children. You will lose the young people from the church. The next generation of the church will be gone!

Interviews with many of the young people who have gone into the cults frequently cite the loss of vibrant life in their church meetings as a reason for leaving them and joining the cult. The cult (at first) seemed to have more joyous spontaneity, more life, more exciting happiness! Later on this cultic joy usually proved to be superficial and a phony cover-up for various types of slavery. Young people were desperately craving joy! Without the joy of the Lord there is imbalance in the church, and its absence will cause people to go to far out extremes searching for it.

Joy is infectious. It is appealing. It draws people to Christ because in His presence is fullness of joy (Psalm 16:11). In Christian churches and in Christian homes, there has got to be this joy. Our constant prayer should be that of David: "Restore unto me the joy of thy salvation" (Psalm 51:12).

Maintaining **BALANCE** *when winds of doctrine blow*

PRAISES TO GOD

To the other essentials of a balanced diet in the spiritual life of a church should be added praise. Unashamed, uninhibited praise, and the giving of thanks to God. The whole Bible is full of directives to praise the Lord.

Praise has always been an essential aspect of the life of God's people in the outworking of their service to God.

"And when the builders laid the foundation of the temple of the Lord, they set the priests in their apparel with trumpets, and the Levites the sons of Asaph with cymbals, to praise the Lord, after the ordinance of David king of Israel.

And they sang together by course in praising and giving thanks unto the Lord; because He is good, for His mercy endureth forever toward Israel.

And the people shouted, when they praised the Lord, because the foundation of the House of the Lord was laid" (Ezra 3:10-11).

The praises of God are meant to be exciting and joyful.

To maintain the dynamic of the early church, we need to maintain a strong spirit of worship and praise. God must be exalted in the midst of the people of God. He is enthroned in our praise (Psalm 22:3). When we involve ourselves in praise and worship we give God His rightful place.

The book of Acts resounds with continual praise and worship. The early Christians did not praise only when they felt like it. They lifted up their "hands as the evening sacrifice" (Psalm 141:2), and offered the "fruit of their lips" as sacrifices continually. Notice that "praising" in Acts 2:47 is again the imperfect Greek tense denoting continual praise.

God has not designed the church meetings as some kind of loose gathering, nor are they meant to be primarily a social event. The first function is to "enter into His gates with thanksgiving, and into His courts with praise (Psalm 100:4).

The praises of God are meant to be exciting and joyful. Not some monotonous chant or repetitious, mournful sound. The word here in the second chapter of Acts is the same word that describes the rejoicing and praise of the shepherds when they saw the Messiah in the manger (Luke 2:12,20). It is used when the multitude marched right into Jerusalem in Christ's triumphal entry (Luke 19:37). It is also used to describe the reaction of the lame man who was just healed by Peter and John (Acts 3:8-9). Those were times of indescribable joy! Take the songs of an angelic Christmas choir, add to them the massive tumult of a multitude in majestic procession, and mix with that the excitement of miraculous

Maintaining
BALANCE
when winds
of
doctrine
blow

healing, and then you will have the kind of praise that should be in the house of the Lord!

SOCIAL IMPACT

Just as Jesus "increased in favour with God <u>and</u> man" (Luke 2:52), so also His church "had favour with all the people" (Acts 2:47).

There are times when nothing you do pleases your enemies. However, to the discerning individuals in society, to the thinking man, a group of people who are following the principles of Christ will be noticed and recognized as beneficial to that society. On the job, the boss will notice something different, "Here is a worker that can be trusted." In politics, "Wow, there's a person of integrity (Daniel 1:9)." In the business world financiers will notice a Christian's honesty (Genesis 39:21). Even if they are not vocal about it, even if they do not admit it, the world takes note and respects the purity and integrity of people who follow the principles of Christ.

A lukewarm church is tasteless and undeserving of favor.

This application of Christian principles and Christian doctrine to daily conduct in the affairs of society is essential to a balanced church. Preaching doctrine is not an end in itself. Doctrines are to be applied to real life situations by those who hear them. The principles in the Bible are to be applied to our society by our church members who are involved in society.

The church must take care that its conduct matches its teaching. Its conduct must not bring reproach upon the gospel, or the name of Christ. Favor from God and man comes when there is a clear line of integrity; when the church is pure and unspotted (James 1:27); when it has righteous standards that are distinguishable from the abnormal customs of the world. Then, and only then, does the church have power and favor. No one respects a compromiser. A lukewarm church is tasteless and undeserving of favor (Revelation 3:16).

On the other hand, think of the potential of men and women who are upright. Noah found grace (favor) in the eyes of the Lord, and life as we know it was preserved from total annihilation (Genesis 6:8). Cornelius had an impeccable life-style as a God-fearer, and through him the door of salvation was opened to the Gentiles. He caught the eye of God (Acts 10:4)! Those who serve in righteousness obtain a good standing in the community, and gain a right to be heard when they speak about the gospel of Christ (I Timothy 3:13). This is confirmed by the Old Testament proverb:

> *"Let not mercy and truth forsake thee; bind them about thy neck; write them upon the table of thine heart; so shalt thou find <u>favour</u> and good understanding in the sight of God and man" (Proverbs 3:3-4; see also Proverbs 22:12).*

Maintaining
BALANCE
when winds
of
doctrine
blow

It was the Christians who were responsible for the end of the gladiator games and senseless, brutal killing of women and children by beasts in coliseums. It was the efforts of Christians that caused the end of the slave trade in the Western world. It was the Christians who sought favor of the rulers to end human sacrifice, polygamy, exposure of children, and cannibalism in the ancient world.[12] It was the Christians who established the moral and social equality of women in human history, and upheld the duty of ministering to the poor and sick.

It was the Christians who were the ones to stand up for the sacredness of marriage by opposing divorce; who stood up for moral purity in society by condemning homosexual practices, fornication, and infidelity. Into the moral vacuum of a dying "civilized paganism" which has fed on brutality, corruption, cruelty, oppression, and sexual chaos, it is the Christian believers and martyrs who have shined as lights in darkness.[13]

Christians need to gain the ear of the people.

"The worst kind of religion is no religion at all, and these men living in ease and luxury, indulging themselves in the amusement of going without religion, may be thankful that they live in lands where the gospel they neglect has tamed the beastliness and ferocity of the men who but for Christianity, might long ago have eaten their carcasses like the South Sea Islanders, or cut off their heads and tanned their hides like the monsters of the French Revolution!"[14]

A historian has noted that Christians standing up for the right of free inquiry and the priesthood of believers during the Reformation was what led to the establishment of liberty and equality as valid principles for nations.[15] The great influence of Christian ideals upon history is so beneficial that it prompted another historian to say that had it not been for the Puritans, political liberty would probably have disappeared from the world!

"If we consider the Puritans in the light of their surroundings as Englishmen of the 17th century and inaugurators of a political movement that was gradually to change for the better the aspect of things <u>all over the earth</u>, we cannot fail to discern the value of that sacred enthusiasm which led them to regard themselves as chosen soldiers of Christ. It was the spirit of the 'Wonder-working Providence' that hurled the tyrant from his throne at Whitehall and prepared the way for the <u>emancipation of modern Europe</u>. No spirit less intense, no spirit nurtured in the contemplation of things terrestrial, could have done it...It is to the fortunate alliance of that fervid religious enthusiasm from the Englishman's love of self-government that <u>our modern freedom owes its existence</u>." (Emphasis is mine.)[16]

Probably the main reason that the Moslem religion was so able to rapidly make

Maintaining **BALANCE** *when winds of doctrine blow*

its conquest across the Mediterranean world in the 600's was that churches at that time had put too large an emphasis on men becoming monks. The withdrawal of Christian men (monks) from society resulted in Christianity losing its influence (favor) in society. The people at large saw no real practical reason for remaining Christian so they turned to the Moslem religion with very little qualms.

So to change the destiny of our countries, Christians need to gain the ear of the people. The church must command respect in the various communities and strata of society in which it exists. And the way it finds this favor in the eyes of its neighbors is to uphold its integrity and righteousness and apply it in every day living.

EVANGELISM WITH COMMITMENT

The last phrase in this second chapter of Acts mentions that the Lord "added to the church daily" all the "saved ones." Back in verse forty-one it mentioned these same words, "the same day there were added..."

Evangelism was at the core of the early church.

Evangelism was at the core of the early church. The last instructions of Jesus were that the disciples should wait to be filled with the Spirit and then go into all the world and preach the gospel to every person. They were to make disciples for Christ all around the world (Matthew 28:19, Mark 16:15, Acts 1:8).

Everywhere the disciples went they preached the good news of the lordship of Christ. And multitudes of people were converted (Acts 5:14, 6:7, 9:42, 11:21, 11:24, 13:43).

Any local church today, if it wishes to remain balanced and receive the blessings of God, must include aggressive evangelism in its spiritual diet. Without this essential ingredient a church will become sluggish, will lose vision, will lose heart, and will pass away within a few generations. The "great commission" cannot be ignored.

The body of the Lord is to be continually reproducing itself. And when the church puts its mind to it, there are dramatic results. Many are "added." Even during adverse conditions such as war, or oppression, or persecution, the Lords adds to His church when Christians get involved. And I believe we are going to see a greater involvement.

Now, notice here that in the second chapter of Acts it says that the new converts were "added to the church." That is, they came together. They identified with a local church. They became committed to a local body.

In the old days, we Pentecostal ministers used to gloat about "being led by the Spirit!" We gave the impression that, "You don't have to be a member of any church. Just be led by the Spirit. Just float." And many people did

Maintaining
BALANCE
when winds
of
doctrine
blow

just that. They were not committed to any thing, any one, or any church.

But it is difficult to imagine the new converts saying, right after Pentecost, "Thanks Peter, for the Holy Spirit. We're going to go out now, and do our own thing." Can you imagine it ever happening?

It did not happen! Once the people were saved and had gone through the Christian new birth, they began to be part of something, they joined themselves to a local body of believers. They were dedicated and committed to the other church members and the elders in leadership.

You see, a church is not simply a crowd that shows up at a meeting. No! The church is family. It is a place where each member receives instruction, discipline, assignments for service, protection, assistance in times of trouble and warm compassion.

The "great commission" cannot be ignored.

New converts will never "grow in grace and in the knowledge of the Lord" on a "come-when-you-want, go-when-you-want, no responsibility, no commitment, do-what-you-want" attitude. They will become anemic, frustrated sheep. And pastors who try to shepherd them will be frustrated also. It is impossible to feed and mature in that kind of situation.

In the letter to the Ephesians, Paul admonishes us to <u>all</u> (plural) come together in the unity of the faith into <u>a</u> (singular) perfect man (4:13). While we all do not lose our unique roles and ministries, yet we are not a bunch of independent souls doing our own thing. We come together into one body. Or, to use another metaphor, we are "builded together" and "framed together" into one house (Ephesians 2:21-22). Individual pieces of lumber do not make a house. God does not want just a lumber pile, but a spiritual people joined together into a "holy habitation" and a "holy temple" (Psalm 92:13, I Peter 2:5).

THE BEST DEFENSE

Someone has said that the best defense is a good offense. To adapt that to our subject, let us say that the best way to keep people from being driven by the nervous Athenian spirit (Acts 17:21) and chasing after new "cotton-candy" doctrines, is to feed the people a balanced spiritual diet, a well-rounded diet that includes all the basic essentials for a healthy Christian life. If we emphasize these basics found in the early church, in the right proportion, we are all going to have churches that maintain their balance. And to me, that's exciting! As a pastor I'm thrilled with the prospect of having a smooth-running church in which all the members mature unto the work of the ministry and edify each other, as well as make an impact for good on society!

Maintaining **BALANCE** *when winds of doctrine blow*

RIGHTEOUS RESULTS

We have already mentioned that if the pastoral leadership lets its congregation get swept away by periodic tides of faddish or popular extremes that hit the shores of Christianity, there are going to be disastrous consequences.

It is exhilarating to know, however, that those churches that are fed a balanced, and fully satisfying, spiritual diet will enjoy many blessings!   This kind of well-pastored congregation has many rewards for which to look forward. The fruit of moderation and balance is very rewarding. Positive fruit will manifest itself in four areas of church life: the individual members, the church families, the pastoral leadership, and the corporate body.

Maintaining **BALANCE** *when winds of doctrine blow*

INDIVIDUAL MEMBERS

Protection Against Deception. Spiritual deception is a major problem today. The interesting fact is that the majority of people drawn into the cults and extreme groups are people who have had some church background! But their experience in church was not a balanced one. It was deficient and lacking in some important areas.

A balanced church that grounds its members in the Word, and in the whole counsel of God, provides a protection against this deception. Surveys taken of many young people show that these young people are not rejecting the Word of God, because they have never been taught the Word of God! They are biblically illiterate. This condition makes them easy picking for fast-talking false apostles. If a person has never seen the true light source, and is walking around in the shadows, everything becomes gray. You cannot tell one gray shadow from another gray shadow. But when you have seen the light, and you are walking in the light (I John 1:6-7) then it is easy to spot darkness! The Word of God is a lamp to keep our feet from stumbling (Psalm 119:105). And a balanced church keeps that lamp shining bright!

The fruit of moderation and balance is very rewarding.

Stability and Steadfastness.   Individuals in a balanced church are going to be stable individuals. Exposed to all the basics of church life, and grounded in the fundamentals of the faith, these will be people you can count on. Established in truth and love, knowledge and wisdom, word and deed, they will always be there ready to serve and minister when needed in the body. Winds of doctrine will only cause these people to drive their roots down further into the bed-rock foundation of the church!

Security. Individuals in a well-rounded church will have a deep sense of security. There is something very satisfying and reassuring about belonging to a church that is orthodox. Sheep crave this security. And if they belong to a church that has an "even keel" it gives them this security.

If the pastor has just run off with half the church treasury, or if a large part of the membership has just broken away to do their own thing, of if there is an uneasy atmosphere of confusion, the sheep are not going to be at ease. They are going to be spending most of their time looking over their shoulder wondering what is going to happen next. They will not be able to relax and put their energies to more constructive use.

But in a balanced church the atmosphere of the kingdom is felt. There is a pervasive spirit of love, peace and joy. The shepherd is faithfully watching over their souls. Their brothers and sisters are right there to give their support. That produces a tremendous feeling of security, and people need this refuge. For some souls who have been abused, have gone through a divorce, or are facing terminal illness or some other of life's tragedies, the church is their only hope for a place of refuge! And how refreshing it is to walk through the doors of a

Maintaining **BALANCE** *when winds of doctrine blow*

church and finally, perhaps for the first time in life, feel secure!

Contentment. The sheep in this kind of church will also feel fulfilled. People who feel fulfilled and who have a sense of purpose will be content. When they are taught in the Word of God, they share the warmth of Christian fellowship, they are involved in the work of the ministry, and they are fulfilling the purpose of God, why would they want to walk away and look for something else? They wouldn't! They are content sheep.

CHURCH FAMILIES

Solid Family Units. A church keeping all the emphases of the Holy Spirit flowing together in a balanced way is going to have solid families. A balanced church always puts a premium on a healthy family unit.

Invariably, any time a person becomes involved in a cult, the first thing they try to do is separate that person from any and all family ties. And if a family joins, they split up that family. The cult leaders want sole authority over each of their lives. Parental authority is not allowed to stand in the way of cultic desires. Children usually become a ward of the commune. Natural affection is broken down.

But God places families in high regard on His list of priorities. The Bible lays stress on

A balanced church always puts a premium on a healthy family unit.

not just the father, or one member, but the whole family coming together and worshipping together.

"...as for me and my house, we will serve the Lord" (Joshua 24:15).

"There was a certain man...a devout man, and one that feared God with all his house..." (Acts 10:1-2).

"And Crispus, the chief ruler of the synagogue, believed on the Lord with all his house..." (Acts 18:8).

In fact, the family is used as one of the prime symbols to describe the church and God's pattern for the church.

"For this cause I bow my knees unto the Father of our Lord Jesus Christ, of whom the whole <u>family</u> in heaven and earth is named" (Ephesians 3:14-15).

The church is patterned after the family, <u>but</u> it is not a replacement for the family. It does not tear down the family, and substitute for it. It does just the opposite. It edifies and solidifies the family unit. All the family units together make up the church. The great covenant God made with Abraham, the "father of the faithful," was that "in him all the families of the earth would be blessed" (Genesis 12:3)! The Christian faith emanating from a balanced church builds solid families.

Maintaining **BALANCE** *when winds of doctrine blow*

**Teaching Families**. These solid families will also be vital teaching families. The parents, grounded in the faith, will teach the next generation and keep the faith moving forward. This is important. It was this quality in Abraham that caught God's eye in choosing him out from all the other men:

> "For I know him, that he will command his children and his household after him, and they shall keep the way of the Lord, to do justice and judgment..." (Genesis 18:19).

The rest of the Bible lends support to this important practice. And a balanced church carries on this tradition:

> "And these words, which I command thee this day, shall be in thine heart; and thou shalt teach them diligently unto thy children, and shalt talk of them when thou sittest in thine house, and when thou walkest by the way, and when thou liest down, and when thou risest up" (Deuteronomy 6:6-7).

> "I will open my mouth in a parable: I will utter dark sayings of old, which we have heard and known, and our fathers have told us.

> We will not hide them from their children, showing to the generation to come the praises of the Lord, and his strength,

God places families in high regard on His list of priorities.

and his wonderful works that He hath done. For he established a testimony in Jacob, and appointed a law in Israel, which he commanded our fathers, that they should make them known to their children;

That the generation to come might know them, even the children which should be born; who should arise and declare them to their children;

That they might set their hope in God, and not forget the works of God, but keep His commandments..." (Psalm 78:2-7).

A whole work of God in a locality can be wiped out in just one generation if the parents simply do not pass on the knowledge of the Lord to their children.[17] A balanced church has the wisdom to keep the Christian faith bubbling with joy "in each house" (Acts 2:46), and from one generation to the next (II Timothy 1:5).

PASTORAL LEADERSHIP

Freedom from stress. There is nothing that causes ministerial burn-out more than the stress brought on by schisms, division, and disputes. It can be a real nightmare counseling shipwrecked members who ran off on some tangent, or spending your time trying to patch up differences between another part of the congregation which is becoming unbalanced in

Maintaining **BALANCE** *when winds of doctrine blow*

still another area. The worry and tension brought on by these who are not trained in moderation and balance can be overwhelming to the pastoral ministry. Many a good man has had to leave the ministry because his people tended to swing from one state of imbalance to another.

But how pleasant it is to the leadership when the church is run on an even keel. When stormy waves come, or gusts of doctrinal emphasis strike, the church just holds on to its steady anchor.

"For God is not unrighteous to forget your work and labour of love, which ye have shewed toward His name, in that ye have ministered to the saints and do minister.

And we desire that every one of you do shew the same diligence to the full assurance of hope unto the end: that ye be not slothful, but followers of them who through faith and patience inherit the promises.

For when God made promise to Abraham, because He could swear by no greater, He sware to Himself, saying, Surely blessing I will bless thee, and multiplying I will multiply thee...

Wherein God, willing more abundantly to shew unto the heirs of promise the

The pastor's problems can upset his wife and also affect his children.

immutability of His counsel, confirmed it by an oath, that by two immutable things, in which it was impossible for God to lie, we might have a strong consolation, who have fled for refuge to lay hold upon the hope set before us, which hope we have as an anchor of the soul, both sure and steadfast, and which entereth into that within the veil;

Whither the forerunner is for us entered, even Jesus, made an high priest forever after the order of Melchizedek" (Hebrews 6:10-20).

The picture given here by the writer to the Hebrews is that of leadership that has trained the church to carry on a mature ministry steadfastly and patiently. It has based its work on the unchanging, "immutable" counsel of God, which has become a strong stabilizing anchor for them. That has been their safety and "refuge" from the storm.

Instead of being tossed around by the storms that come (and in the ministry they do come), being dashed upon the rocks and shipwrecked, and having to start all over again from scratch, this church just keeps pressing on. The leadership does not have to go back and start over teaching the basic fundamentals because its members are not tossed about by the latest movement (5:12-6:3). Its members do not keep "falling away" and they are not continually having to "repent" again and again.

Maintaining **BALANCE** *when winds of doctrine blow*

And that is a blessing and a big relief to the leadership. Instead of worrying and being overcome by stress, the oversight can get on with the program!

Peace in the Pastor's Family. No one knows how much stress a minister is going through more than his family does. The pastor's problems can upset his wife and also affect his children. There have been some serious tragedies in this area. I am quite sure we all could relate some incidence of hurt families because of church squabbles.

But what a blessing it is to the pastor's and elders' families to experience the peace and tranquility that comes from a smooth-running, even keeled body of believers! The stability and steadfastness of the congregation carries on over to the families and enhances their emotional and psychological health. That is a great blessing. It is hard for a minister to give himself fully to his work when back home there are emotional problems, confusion and anxieties. But it is a delight when the pastor's family is uplifted and supported by the congregation of a stable church!

Fulfillment of Purpose and Vision. At the end of our lives we all want to have a deep sense of accomplishment. We do not want to feel that our lives and efforts have been wasted. We receive that contentment only when we see our dreams and vision for the local church fulfilled. A stable, balanced

We do not want to feel that our lives and efforts have been wasted.

church provides the best chance for this to happen.

When the congregation is given a balanced spiritual diet that keeps all the areas of church life flowing in moderation, and when they realize their leadership does not run after every new thing that comes along, then they can have great confidence in them. They are willing to get behind their oversight to accomplish the vision that has been given. They have a zeal and a motivation to see things done, because they know it is not a "fly-by-night" project. They know that they are not wasting their time, money or energy. Their labor of love is going to have eternal value.

This unified zeal to carry on the work of the Lord swells the heart of all pastors with an undying gratitude and thankfulness. It means that they will accomplish the vision.

THE CORPORATE BODY

Strong, Enduring Church. The fruit of balance is, above all, a strong permanent, enduring church. I have seen some churches start up in a city. Like a mushroom, they pop up over night. They flourish for a while, living on some popular religious craze. Then you look around and they are gone. A year later here's another "flash in the pan" church based on another new popular movement.

Maintaining **BALANCE** *when winds of doctrine blow*

Personally, I am interested in strong, enduring churches, because a church represents the precious lives of people. It is not just an organization, it is people who love God. It might take a little longer to have a "permanent" church, but that is alright with me. It is normal to "grow" slowly.

Effective Evangelism. A well-balanced church has lasting fruit. People are not just attracted to the church by a novel doctrine, or the spectacular, or by extravagant promises. But they are grounded in the Word. They are nurtured like young babes. They are steadily discipled. They are watched over, cared for, counseled, plugged into the family, involved in worship, and matured.

This can only happen if the church is a strong base for pediatric care, providing a well-rounded service. New converts are young babies. And if you bring them into a weak house, or a house that is out of balance by extremes or schisms, they will die. They will filter right back into the world. And we do not want that. We all want fruit that remains. That is our cause for rejoicing at the day of the Lord (II Corinthians 1:14, Philippians 2:16, 4:1).

We all want fruit that remains.

Reproduced Ministry. A church in balance will not only produce mature Christians from new converts, but some of those will go on to become full-time ministers. There will be an excitement in the House of God that will not only produce righteous living, but it will also produce new ministries (II Timothy 2:2, contrast Hebrews 5:12).

In our church, as long as we majored in just one aspect of the gospel, that is the deliverance ministry, we never reproduced a single minister. For fifteen years as a "deliverance" church not one single minister came up. That used to really bother me. But when God began to change us and bring us into understanding and the balance of the Word of God, we saw many of our sons and daughters set themselves aside for leadership ministry.

Now we have a Bible College that educates and trains pastoral ministers, music ministers, and lay leaders for our society.[18] That's exciting. It's exciting to reproduce yourself. But a church way out in extremes will become sterile. It will not produce quality Christian leaders.

Variety of Ministries. A balanced church that is functioning as the Body of Christ was designed will have a wide variety of ministries. If you are a "deliverance church" usually just the deliverance ministers are allowed to function. If you are a "faith church" just those who teach faith or have the gift of faith are in the forefront. If you are a "teaching church" teaching ministers are developed and promoted.

Maintaining **BALANCE** *when winds of doctrine blow*

But a balanced church that is functioning like the body it was meant to be, will have a whole variety of ministers (I Corinthians 12). All the gifts to the church will be allowed to function, including apostles, prophets, evangelists, pastors, teachers, helps, those with the gifts of healings, miracles, prophecy, those with the tremendous ministry of hospitality, those skilled in working with the young of the flock or the senior citizens. Everyone will be released to work in the calling and ministry God has given them.

And that's exciting. When all the different types of ministry are at work, then all the needs of the people are met. Not just some, but all. Each and every joint and ligament is supporting the other which results in the edification of the whole body (Ephesians 4:16).

Influence in Society. A strong, permanent church that is moving forward in God will soon be recognized in its society as a force to be reckoned with. It will have an impact for good upon that society. It will be respected and find favor.

The church has a powerful message.

This does not mean there will not be times of persecution and conflict. On the contrary, when Christians stand up for righteousness and justice, there is often confrontation. But even in the midst of the "battle" there is respect and influence that a church commands.

"The Pharisees therefore said among themselves, Perceive ye how ye prevail nothing? Behold, the world is gone after Him" (John 12:19)!

"And he taught daily in the temple. But the chief priests and the scribes and the chief of the people sought to destroy Him, and could not find what they might do: for all the ·people were very attentive to hear Him [lit. "hanged on to Him]" (Luke 19:47-48).

"These that have turned the world upside down are come thither also" (Acts 17:6b).

The church has a powerful message. It can shake an evil culture or society to its boots. It is a city set high upon a hill that can be seen and that can serve as a reference point for wandering souls. It is like salt that affects everything with which it comes into contact. Its members have the potential of reaching into every stratum of society and influencing it for righteousness!

THE FRUIT OF BALANCE

The apostolic church was a tremendously successful, growing church. It reached into every area of Roman, Greek, and Jewish society and influenced it for good. It expanded throughout the Roman empire and eventually brought it to its knees.

Maintaining **BALANCE** *when winds of doctrine blow*

But the early church was a balanced church. It kept all the spiritual emphases flowing in perfect harmony and balance. And that was powerful. It brought glory to God and drew favor from all the people (Acts 2:47).

There is no reason why each of our modern day local churches cannot experience the same wholeness, power and influence. We all have that same potential.

But it must come about by the same method. Maintaining moderation, steadfastness and stability through balance. And to me, as a pastor who wants to rejoice at the coming of the Lord because of much fruit, this is a blessing. This is important to me. But it is also very exciting because in this I see a great potential for all of us as ministers, and for all our local churches!

There is no reason why modern day churches cannot experience wholeness, power and influence.

END NOTES

1. For a further discussion of team ministry see a book entitled <u>Team Ministry</u> by the same author.

2. p. A2, Rushworth M. Kidder, "Melting Pot or Salad Bowl?", Oregonian, May 2, 1987.

3. This is the central devastating error in "sex education" classes in public high schools: they dispense information and knowledge of an intimate nature, but are pitifully lacking in teaching discernment and wisdom which provide an ethic for correct conduct in these matters!

4. p. 405-406, Augustus Neander, <u>History of the Christian Religion and Church</u>, 3rd ed., Stanford & Swords, NY 1853).

5. p. 3, Personal Freedom Outreach (anti-cult newsletter), January-March, 1987, St. Louis, Missouri.

6. p. 405, J.H. Thayer, <u>Greek-English Lexicon</u>, Zondervan, June 1974.

Maintaining **BALANCE** *when winds of doctrine blow*

7.   Archaeology has recently discovered many "immersion baths" throughout Judea, but especially in Jerusalem near the temple area. (Hebrew, <u>miqva'ot</u>, sing.) These are large hewn pools of water with steps leading down to them, and they are deep enough for complete immersion of an individual. (p. 52-59, William Sanford LaSor, "Discovering what Jewish Miqva'ot Can Tell Us About Christian Baptism", Archaeology Review, Jan-Feb, 1987).

8.   For example. According to a review of the book, <u>The Mormon Corporate Empire</u>, by John Heinerman, a Mormon anthropologist, and Anson Shupe, a Methodist sociologist, the Mormons have engaged in a slick public relations effort to project a mythological image of "benevolence, wholesomeness and uprightness."

9.   See Dick Iverson, <u>Team Ministry</u>, Bible Temple Publishing, 1984.

10.   A lot of scandals in our day in churches and religious organizations are the result, to a large degree, of "solo ministries." Individual ministers without the checks and balances of team ministers, and who are unaccountable to anyone. When these "solo ministers" succumb to lust, greed, or fraud, it snowballs unchecked

until thousands of innocent people are affected. That is sad. It doesn't need to happen. It could easily be avoided if we would stick to biblical principles!

11. The breaking of bread and eating food here is taken by some to mean the Lord's Supper. However, Luke has already mentioned the Lord's Supper in Acts 2:42, and breaking of bread does refer to the common meal in other scriptures: the feeding of the 5,000 (Matthew 14:19), the feeding of the 4,000 (Matthew 15:36), Paul eating on ship (Acts 27:35). I don't think Luke is repeating himself in this list of foundational principles of church life. The everyday, common duties of the believers were a joyous celebration of life!

12. p. 99, William E Gladstone (British statesman), Correspondence on Church and Religion, London 1910.

13. pp. 598-602, Will Durant, Caesar and Christ, Simon and Shulster, N.Y. 1944.

14. p. 296-297, James Russell Lowell, quoted in David G. Mears, The Deathless Book, Boston, 1888.

Maintaining **BALANCE** *when winds of doctrine blow*

15. p. 7, G.P. Gooch (historian) quoted in English Democratic Ideas in the Seventeenth Century, 2nd ed., 1927.

16. p. 37-46, John Fiske (no Christian himself), The Beginnings of New England, Boston, 1889.

17. For a full development of the importance of the family in the local church see, Dick Iverson et al. Restoring the Family: Principles of Family Life, Bible Temple Publishing, Portland, Oregon, 1979.

18. For a brochure or catalog describing Portland Bible College and its programs, write Portland Bible College, 9201 NE Fremont, Portland, Oregon 97220.

DATE DUE